Introducing Microsoft SQL Server 2014

ROSS MISTRY
STACIA MISNER

PUBLISHED BY
Microsoft Press
A Division of Microsoft Corporation
One Microsoft Way
Redmond, Washington 98052-6399

Library of Congress Control Number: 2014934033
ISBN: 978-0-7356-8475-1

Printed and bound in the United States of America.

Second Printing: April 2014

Microsoft Press books are available through booksellers and distributors worldwide. If you need support related to this book, email Microsoft Press Book Support at mspinput@microsoft.com. Please tell us what you think of this book at http://www.microsoft.com/learning/booksurvey.

Microsoft and the trademarks listed at http://www.microsoft.com/en-us/legal/intellectualproperty/Trademarks/EN-US.aspx are trademarks of the Microsoft group of companies. All other marks are property of their respective owners.

The example companies, organizations, products, domain names, email addresses, logos, people, places, and events depicted herein are fictitious. No association with any real company, organization, product, domain name, email address, logo, person, place, or event is intended or should be inferred.

This book expresses the author's views and opinions. The information contained in this book is provided without any express, statutory, or implied warranties. Neither the authors, Microsoft Corporation, nor its resellers, or distributors will be held liable for any damages caused or alleged to be caused either directly or indirectly by this book.

Acquisitions Editor: Devon Musgrave
Developmental Editor: Devon Musgrave
Project Editor: Carol Dillingham
Editorial Production: Flyingspress and Rob Nance
Technical Reviewer: Stevo Smocilac; Technical Review services provided by Content Master, a member of CM Group, Ltd.
Copyeditor: John Pierce
Indexer: Lucie Haskins
Cover: Twist Creative • Seattle

I dedicate this book to my Kyanna and Kaden. Follow your passions, and never let anyone hold you back. And to the next chapter in the game of life, "Return of the Autumn Wind."

—Ross Mistry

I dedicate this book to my SQL family all around the world. You all bring a lot of enthusiasm and passion of your own to this profession, which inspires me and spurs me on to learn more so that I can share more. Thanks to each of you for what you give to me.

—Stacia Misner

Contents at a glance

Contents

Chapter 6 Big data solutions   101

What do you think of this book? We want to hear from you!

Microsoft is interested in hearing your feedback so we can continually improve our books and learning resources for you. To participate in a brief online survey, please visit:

microsoft.com/learning/booksurvey

Introduction

Microsoft SQL Server 2014 is the next generation of Microsoft's information platform, with new features that deliver faster performance, expand capabilities in the cloud, and provide powerful business insights. In this book, we explain how SQL Server 2014 incorporates in-memory technology to boost performance in online transactional processing (OLTP) and data-warehouse solutions. We also describe how it eases the transition from on-premises solutions to the cloud with added support for hybrid environments. SQL Server 2014 continues to include components that support analysis, although no major new features for business intelligence were included in this release. However, several advances of note have been made in related technologies such as Microsoft Excel 2013, Power BI for Office 365, HDInsight, and PolyBase, and we describe these advances in this book as well.

Who should read this book?

This book is for anyone who has an interest in SQL Server 2014 and wants to understand its capabilities. Many new improvements have been made to SQL Server 2014, but in a book of this size we cannot cover every improvement in its entirety—or cover every feature that distinguishes SQL Server from other databases or SQL Server 2014 from previous versions. Consequently, we assume that you have some familiarity with SQL Server already. You might be a database administrator (DBA), an application developer, a business intelligence solution architect, a power user, or a technical decision maker. Regardless of your role, we hope that you can use this book to discover the features in SQL Server 2014 that are most beneficial to you.

Assumptions

We assume that you have at least a minimal understanding of SQL Server from both a database administrator's perspective and a business-intelligence perspective, including a general understanding of Microsoft Excel, which is often used with SQL Server. In addition, having a basic understanding of Windows Azure is helpful for getting the most from the topics associated with private, public, and hybrid-cloud solutions.

Who should not read this book

As mentioned earlier, the purpose of this book is to provide readers with a high-level preview of the capabilities and features of SQL Server 2014. This book is not intended to be a step-by-step, comprehensive guide.

How is this book organized?

SQL Server 2014, like its predecessors, is more than a database engine. It is a collection of components that you can implement separately or as a group to form a scalable, cloud-ready information platform. In broad terms, this platform is designed for two purposes: to help you manage data and to help you deliver business intelligence. Accordingly, we divided this book into two parts to focus on the new capabilities in each of those areas.

Part 1, "Database administration," is written with the database administrator (DBA) in mind and introduces readers to the numerous innovations in SQL Server 2014. Chapter 1, "SQL Server 2014 editions and engine enhancements," discusses the key enhancements affiliated with availability, scalability, performance, manageability, security, and programmability. It then outlines the different SQL Server 2014 editions; hardware and software requirements; and installation, upgrade, and migration strategies. In Chapter 2, "In-Memory OLTP investments," readers learn about the new in-memory feature that provides significant performance gains for OLTP workloads. Chapter 3, "High-availability, hybrid-cloud, and backup enhancements," aims to bring readers up to date on these important capabilities that are fully integrated into SQL Server 2014 and Windows Azure.

Part 2, "Business intelligence development," is for readers who need to understand how SQL Server 2014 and related technologies can be used to build analytical solutions that enable deeper insights through the combination of all types of data—big or small, structured or unstructured. Chapter 4, "Exploring self-service BI in Microsoft Excel 2013," introduces add-ins for Excel that expand beyond the data mash-up capabilities of Power Pivot by supporting the abilities to find and manipulate data, create rich interactive visualizations, and explore location-based data on a 3-D map. Chapter 5, "Introducing Power BI for Office 365," shows you not only how to move Excel workbooks to the cloud for centralized access in SharePoint Online, but also how to use Power BI features online to manage workbooks and even get answers to natural-language questions from published workbooks. Chapter 6, "Big data solutions," explores technologies that extend the reach of analytical tools beyond relational data to Hadoop by using Microsoft HDInsight in the cloud or PolyBase on-premises.

Conventions and features in this book

This book presents information using the following conventions, which are designed to make the information more readable and easy to follow:

- Step-by-step instructions consist of a series of tasks, presented as numbered steps (1, 2, and so on) listing each action you must take to complete a task.

- Boxed elements with labels such as "Note" provide additional information.

- Text that you type (apart from code blocks) appears in bold.

- Transact-SQL code is provided to help you further understand specific examples.

Pre-release software

To help you become familiar with SQL Server 2014 as soon as possible after its release, we wrote this book using examples that work with the Community Technology Preview (CTP) 2 version of the product. Consequently, the final version might include new features, and features we discuss might change or disappear. Refer to the "What's New in SQL Server 2014" topic in Books Online for SQL Server at *http://msdn.microsoft.com/ en-us/library/bb500435(v=sql.120).aspx* for the most up-to-date list of changes to the product. Be aware that you might also notice some minor differences between the CTP 2 version of the product and the descriptions and screen shots that we provide.

Acknowledgments

First, I would like to thank my colleagues at Microsoft Press for providing me with another writing opportunity, which allows me to enhance the careers of many data-platform professionals around the world. Special kudos go out to Devon Musgrave, Colin Lyth, Anne Hamilton, Karen Szall, Carol Dillingham, John Pierce, Stevo Smocilac, Rob Nance, Carrie Wicks, and Lucie Haskins. The publishing team's support throughout this engagement is much appreciated.

Second, this book would not have been possible without support from colleagues on the SQL Server team who provided introductions, strategic technology guidance, technical reviews, and edits. I would like to thank Sunil Agarwal, Luis Carlos Vargas Herring, Sethu Srinivasan, Darmadi Komo, and Luis Daniel Soto Maldonado.

Third, I would like to acknowledge Shirmattie Seenarine for assisting me on another Microsoft Press title. Shirmattie's hard work, contributions, edits, and rewrites are much appreciated. And to my author partner, Stacia Misner, I want to thank you for once again doing an excellent job on the business intelligence part of this book.

Finally, I would like to thank my mentors at Microsoft and my amazing Canadian team at the Microsoft Technology Center who have allowed me to achieve success north of the border.

–Ross Mistry

Here I am collaborating yet again with Ross and thank him for the opportunity. Like Ross, I appreciate very much the team at Microsoft Press that helped us through the process of creating this book. Various other people also help behind the scenes by answering questions and exploring alternative options for working with the new technologies available for the Microsoft business-intelligence stack. At Microsoft, I thank Cristian Petculescu, Ed Price, Igor Peeve, and Blair Neumann. In the SQL Server community, I have Joey D'Antoni and Aaron Nelson to thank for their willingness to answer random questions at odd hours that ultimately helped me save much time during the writing of this book.

–Stacia Misner

Errata & book support

We've made every effort to ensure the accuracy of this book. Any errors that have been reported since this book was published are listed at:

http://aka.ms/IntroSQLServer2014/errata

If you discover an error that is not already listed, please submit it to us at the same page. If you need additional support, email Microsoft Press Book Support at *mspinput@microsoft.com*.

Please note that product support for Microsoft software and hardware is not offered through the previous addresses. For help with Microsoft software or hardware, go to *http://support.microsoft.com*.

We want to hear from you

At Microsoft Press, your satisfaction is our top priority, and your feedback our most valuable asset. Please tell us what you think of this book at:

http://aka.ms/tellpress

The survey is short, and we read every one of your comments and ideas. Thanks in advance for your input!

Stay in touch

Let's keep the conversation going! We're on Twitter: *http://twitter.com/MicrosoftPress.*

Database administration

CHAPTER 1

SQL Server 2014 editions and engine enhancements

SQL Server 2014, the latest complete information platform from Microsoft, embodies the new era of Microsoft's Cloud OS, which provides organizations and customers with one consistent platform for infrastructure, apps and data that span customer data centers, hosting service-provider data centers, and the Microsoft public cloud. The benefits that customers experience with a consistent platform include common development, management, data, identity, and virtualization, no matter where an application is being run.

SQL Server 2014 also offers organizations the opportunity to efficiently protect, unlock, and scale their data across the desktop, mobile devices, data centers, and a private, public, or hybrid cloud. Furthermore, SQL Server 2014 builds on the success of SQL Server 2012 by making a strong impact on organizations worldwide with significant new capabilities that are tightly aligned to the trends transforming the IT industry, including Microsoft's Cloud OS. SQL Server provides mission-critical performance for the most demanding database applications while delivering the highest forms of security, scalability, high availability, and support. SQL Server 2014's mission is to deliver faster insights into big data, small data—all data—and, most importantly, deliver business intelligence in a consumable manner through familiar tools such as Microsoft Excel.

Finally, SQL Server 2014 enables new unique hybrid-cloud solutions based on the Cloud OS. These solutions can positively affect an organization's bottom line and allow an organization to create innovative solutions for its database applications. Figure 1-1 shows the mission statement for SQL Server 2014, based on three pillars.

SQL Server 2014 and the Data Platform

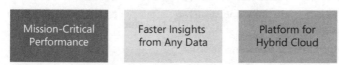

FIGURE 1-1 SQL Server 2014, a cloud-ready information platform.

This chapter examines the new features, capabilities, and editions of SQL Server 2014 from a database administrator's perspective. It also describes hardware and software requirements and installation strategies.

SQL Server 2014 enhancements for database administrators

The organizations of today are looking for a trusted, cost-effective, and scalable database platform that offers mission-critical confidence, breakthrough insights, and flexible cloud-based offerings. These organizations regularly face changing business conditions in the global economy and numerous challenges to remaining competitive, such as gaining valuable business insights, using the right information at the right time, and working successfully within budget constraints.

In addition, organizations must be fluid because new and important trends regularly change the way software is developed and deployed. Some of these trends focus on in-memory databases that can improve performance and efficiency, a capability that has most likely been influenced by the dramatic drop in the cost of memory. Another important trend sweeping over IT is the adoption of cloud computing by customers who require an infrastructure that provides a generational leap in agility, elasticity, and scalability across a set of shared resources with more automation of cloud services and self-service provisioning. Last but not least is the data-explosion trend, where discussions about storage capacity naturally involve the word *zettabytes*. Customers want to gain new insights about their businesses faster, so they are analyzing larger data sets, both internal and external. These new insights are helping customers obtain a competitive edge, but they are also leading to massive volumes of data.

Microsoft has made major investments in SQL Server 2014 as a whole. The new features and capabilities that should interest database administrators are introduced in this chapter, including availability, backup and restore, scalability, performance, security, manageability, programmability, and the platform for the hybrid cloud. Other chapters in this book offer a deeper explanation of the major technology investments.

Availability enhancements

A tremendous number of high-availability enhancements were added to SQL Server 2012, which increased both the confidence that organizations have in their databases and the maximum uptime for those databases. Microsoft built on this work with new high-availability enhancements in SQL Server 2014.

AlwaysOn Availability Groups

In SQL Server 2012, AlwaysOn Availability Groups was the most highly anticipated feature related to the Database Engine for DBAs. This high-availability and disaster-recovery capability provided protection by allowing one or more databases to fail over as a single unit. Shared storage was not needed, and replicas could be leveraged to offload backups and reporting workloads from the primary.

Enhancements in SQL Server 2014 have given databases even better data redundancy, protection, and availability. First, the maximum number of secondary replicas has increased from four to eight. This change allows organizations to further offload read-only operations such as reporting and backups to additional secondary replicas. The additional secondary replicas can also be placed in more data centers for higher levels of protection and disaster recovery. Moreover, with SQL Server 2014, the secondary replicas have been enhanced and can be used for read-only operations even in the case of network failures or loss of quorum between replicas. Second, whether a manual or an automatic failover is performed, the operation no longer needs to fail over databases one at a time. Numerous databases can now fail over simultaneously, which increases availability.

Finally, SQL Server 2014 introduces the Add Azure Replica wizard for organizations looking to create a secondary replica that is stored in Windows Azure, Microsoft's public cloud. (See Figure 1-2.) Placing a secondary replica in Windows Azure is a great way for an organization to achieve additional disaster-recovery protection in the unlikely event that all data centers hosting its secondary replicas become unavailable.

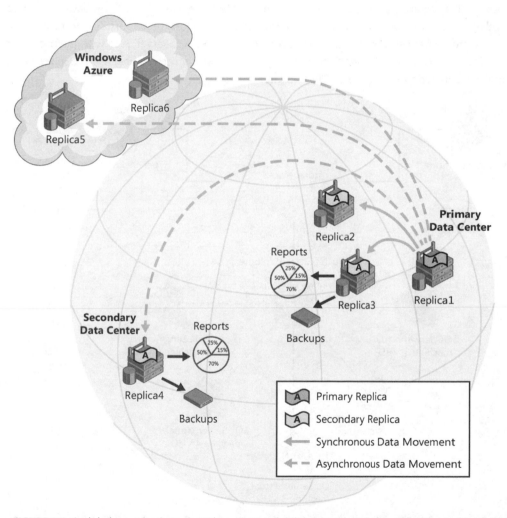

FIGURE 1-2 A global organization using AlwaysOn Availability Groups, including Windows Azure, to achieve high availability and disaster recovery.

In Figure 1-2, company X is an organization with a global presence. It achieves both high availability and disaster recovery for mission-critical databases by using AlwaysOn Availability Groups. Secondary replicas are placed in data centers around the world, including in Windows Azure, and are being used to offload reporting and backups.

AlwaysOn Failover Cluster Instances (FCI)

AlwaysOn Failover Cluster Instances (FCIs) is a feature that provides superior instance-level protection by using Windows Server Failover Clustering and shared storage. Traditionally, each SQL Server failover cluster instance required at least one logical unit number (LUN) because the LUN was the unit of failover. This requirement imposed a significant limitation because when a database administrator ran out of drive letters or mount points, the administrator also lost the opportunity to host any more failover cluster instances. This anomaly has been addressed in SQL Server 2014 with the use of the Cluster Shared Volumes (CSVs) feature, as shown in Figure 1-3, which requires fewer LUNs. As a note, this feature is included in Windows 2012 and later releases.

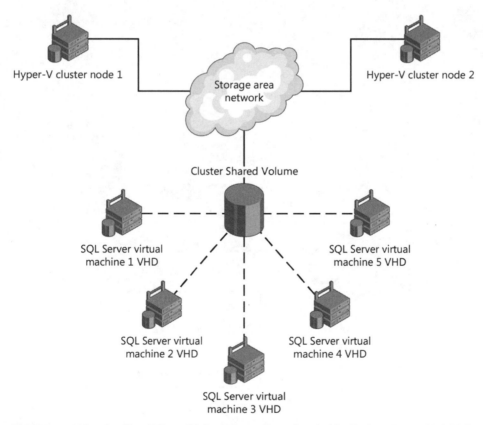

FIGURE 1-3 Using the Cluster Shared Volume feature associated with Windows Server 2012 R2 for storing SQL Server 2014 virtual machines.

CSVs reduce the number of LUNs (disks) required for SQL Server clustered instances because many failover cluster instances can use a single CSV LUN and can fail over without causing the other FCIs on the same LUN to also fail over. Finally, new dynamic management views introduced in SQL Server 2014 help administrators troubleshoot and return information pertaining to FCIs.

Backup and restore enhancements

Regardless of how many database replicas an organization has within its enterprise, there is still a need to protect data with backups. Hence, Microsoft continued its investments in backup and recovery to protect data with SQL Server 2014. The new enhancements include the following:

- **SQL Server Managed Backups to Windows Azure** Backups in SQL Server 2014 natively support the Windows Azure Blob storage service for simplifying backups to the cloud. Hybrid-cloud backups reduce capital expenditures (CAPEX) and operational expenditures (OPEX) and improve disaster recovery for an organization's backups because the backups stored in the Windows Azure cloud are automatically replicated to multiple data centers around the world. The process to exploit this new enhancement is fairly straightforward. First, create a Windows Azure storage account and a blob container, and then generate a SQL Server credential that will be used to store security information and access the Windows Azure storage account. Finally, create a backup that will use the Windows Azure Blob storage service.

- **SQL Server backups to URLs** SQL Server backups have been updated to use URLs as one of the destination options when backups are performed with SQL Server Management Studio. Backups are stored in Windows Azure because the Windows Azure Blob storage service is used. Previously, only Transact-SQL, PowerShell, and SQL Server Management Objects (SMO) were supported when using SQL Server 2012 SP1 CU2 and later. A database backup to a URL destination is depicted in Figure 1-4.

- **Encryption for backups** For years, DBAs have been asking for the ability to natively encrypt data while creating a backup. This task can now be performed in SQL Server 2014 by specifying an encryption algorithm and an encryptor—a certificate or an asymmetric key—to secure the encryption key. The industry standard encryption algorithms that are supported include AES 128, AES 192, AES 256, and Triple DES. Encrypted backups are supported in Windows Azure storage or on-premises.

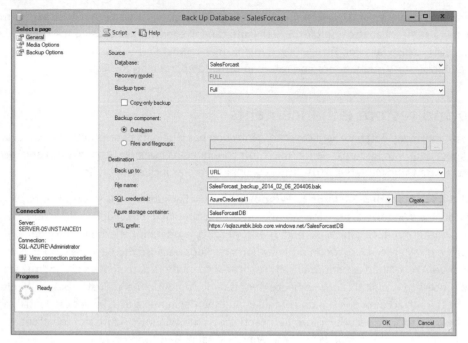

FIGURE 1-4 Backing up a database to an Azure storage container by using a URL prefix.

Scalability and performance enhancements

The SQL Server product group made sizable investments to improve scalability and performance associated with the SQL Server Database Engine. Some of the main enhancements allow organizations to improve their SQL Server workloads, especially when using Windows Server 2012 or later releases:

- **In-Memory OLTP** In-Memory OLTP (project code name Hekaton) is considered the most important feature release and investment in SQL Server 2014. This new feature is fully integrated into the Database Engine component. Databases were originally designed to reside on disk because of the high costs associated with procuring memory. This situation has since changed, due mainly to the significant drop in price for memory. It is now possible for most OLTP databases to fit into memory, which reduces I/O expense, and in turn increases transaction speed performance. To date, organizations testing In-Memory OLTP have reported promising numbers: transaction speeds improved up to 30 times that of their past performance. As with any new capability, mileage will vary, and the best performance gains have been achieved when the business logic resides in the database and not in the applications.

- **Computing resources** At the heart of the Microsoft Cloud OS vision, Windows Server 2012 R2 offers a tremendous amount of computing resources to provide scale for large, mission-critical databases not only in a physical environment but also in a virtual environment. Windows Server 2012 R2 supports up to 2,048 logical processers for a Hyper-V host, which can handle the largest database applications. In a virtual environment you can use up to 64 virtual CPUs, up to 1 terabyte (TB) of memory, and up to 64 TB of virtual disk capability for each Hyper-V virtual guest. In addition, you now have up to 64 nodes in a SQL Server cluster and up to 8,000 virtual machines within a Hyper-V cluster. Enterprise scale on this magnitude has never been achieved before.

- **Scale networking**   Windows Server 2012 R2 introduced many new capabilities in the area of virtual networking that bolster the SQL Server experience. Network virtualization provides a needed layer of abstraction, which allows SQL Server workloads to be moved from one data center to another. NIC teaming, which was introduced with Windows Server 2012, still exists and can be used to provide fault tolerance by enabling multiple network interfaces to work together as a team. Finally, SMB Multichannel and Network Quality of Service (QoS) can be used in conjunction with SQL Server to improve database application availability over physical and virtual networks by ensuring that multiple paths are available to application shares and that sufficient available bandwidth is reserved for the application.

- **Scale storage**   Windows Server 2012 introduced Storage Spaces, a feature that was enhanced in Windows Server 2012 R2. Storage spaces allow database administrators to take advantage of sophisticated virtualization enhancements to the storage stack that can distribute or tier SQL Server workloads across storage pools. For example, high-capacity spinning disks can be used to store less frequently used data, while high-speed solid-state disks can be used to store more frequently used data. Windows Server 2012 R2 recognizes the tiers and optimizes them by placing hot data in the fastest tier and less-utilized data in lower tiers, improving performance without increasing costs.

- **Resource Governor enhancements**   In previous versions of SQL Server, it was possible to pool CPU and memory to manage SQL Server workloads and system-resource consumption. In SQL Server 2014, I/O has been added to Resource Governor, which lets I/O be pooled and tiered following an organization's criteria. This ensures greater scale and performance predictability for your SQL Server workloads, especially when running applications in private clouds and environments managed by hosting organizations.

- **Buffer pool extension**   Buffer pool extension enables integration of a nonvolatile random-access-memory extension with the Database Engine buffer pool to significantly improve I/O throughput. Solid-state drives (SSDs) would be considered nonvolatile random access memory, which would be added to the SQL Server system to improve query performance. Benefits that can be achieved when you use buffer pool extension include increased random I/O throughput, reduced I/O latency, increased transaction throughput, improved read performance with a larger buffer pool, and a caching architecture that can take advantage of present and future low-cost memory drives.

- **Sysprep enhancements**   SQL Server 2014 supports new functionality in Sysprep, which allows you to fully support deployments of clustered SQL Server instances. This capability reduces deployment time for SQL Server failover clusters and is great for building private or public clouds.

- **Columnstore enhancements**   Columnstore indexes are used to accelerate query performance for data warehousing that primarily performs bulk loads. In the previous version of

SQL Server, tables that had columnstore indexes could not be updated. In the past, you had to drop the index, perform the update, and then rebuild the index, or use partition switching or two tables—one with a columnstore index and another for updating—and then use UNION ALL queries to return data. As you can imagine, this could be challenging from an administrative perspective. With SQL Server 2014, in-memory columnstore has been modified to support updateable operations such as inserts, updates, and deletes.

Security enhancements

Approximately a decade has passed since Microsoft initiated its trustworthy computing initiative. Compared with other major database players in the industry, SQL Server has had the best track record since then, with the least number of vulnerabilities and exposures. Based on results from an April 2013 study conducted by the National Institute of Standards and Technology (NIST), shown in Figure 1-5, SQL Server led the way five years in a row as the least-vulnerable database among the top data platforms tracked. Moreover, it is currently the most-utilized database in the world, with 42 percent of market share. (Source: ITIC 2013: "SQL Server Delivers Industry-Leading Security.")

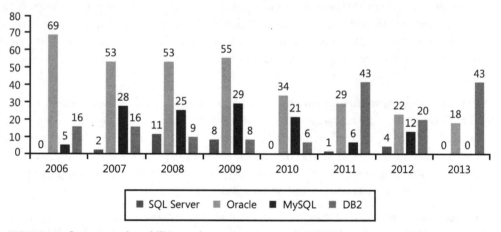

FIGURE 1-5 Common vulnerabilities and exposures reported to NIST from January 2006 to January 2013.

With SQL Server 2014, the product continues to expand its solid foundation to deliver enhanced security and compliance within the database platform. By splitting the database administrator role from the system administrator role and allowing organizations to further customize the rights of each DBA or system administrator, greater compliance and security can be achieved. Here is a snapshot of some of the enhanced enterprise-ready security capabilities and controls that enable organizations to meet strict compliance policies and regulations:

- Redefined engineering security process

- CC certification at high assurance level

- Enhanced separation of duty

- Transparent data encryption (TDE)

- Encryption key management

- Support for Windows Server Core

A new set of explicit server-level and database-level permissions for securables have been introduced in SQL Server 2014 to further enhance access and security:

- **CONNECT ANY DATABASE**   A server-level permission that grants a login the ability to connect to all databases that currently exist and to any new databases that might be created in the future.

- **IMPERSONATE ANY LOGIN**   Another new server-level permission, IMPERSONATE ANY LOGIN allows a middle-tier process to impersonate the account of clients connecting to it as it connects to databases.

- **SELECT ALL USER SECURABLES**   When granted, this new server-level permission allows a login to view data in all databases that the user can connect to.

- **ALTER ANY DATABASE EVENT SESSION**   Unlike the other permissions listed here, ALTER ANY DATABASE EVENT SESSION is a database-level permission. It is typically used to give a role the ability to read metadata associated with a database for monitoring purposes. A perfect example would be Microsoft System Center Operations Manager agents used to proactively monitor a SQL Server database.

Platform for hybrid cloud

SQL Server 2014 empowers a diverse set of hybrid-cloud opportunities that can reduce both capital and operational expenditures for an organization. These include backing up to the cloud, extending high availability to the cloud, hybrid application development, and improved on-premises disaster recovery. Let's review the different types of hybrid-cloud solutions that organizations can take advantage of:

- **Deploy a database to SQL Server in a Windows Azure Virtual Machine**   A new wizard in SQL Server 2014 allows a DBA to use SQL Server Management Studio to seamlessly deploy and transition a database from an on-premises deployment to a Windows Azure Virtual Machine. Windows Azure Virtual Machines are an Infrastructure-as-a-Service (IaaS) offering included in Windows Azure. The implementation is based on a few simple steps:

  1. Specify the source connection settings such as the SQL Server instance, database name, and temporary location for backup files.

  2. Provide Windows Azure sign-in credentials that include a management certificate.

  3. Enter information for the Windows Azure Virtual Machine or, if you plan on deploying your database to an existing Windows Azure Virtual Machine, provide the DNS name for the cloud service and the credentials for the virtual machine and SQL Server instance.

- **Deploy a database to Windows Azure SQL Database**   Another new feature in SQL Server 2014 allows a DBA to easily deploy an on-premises database to Windows Azure SQL Database. Windows Azure SQL Database is a relational-database service in the Windows Azure Platform-as-a-Service (PaaS) environment. The wizard used in this type of deployment can also be used to move databases from Windows Azure SQL Database to an on-premises SQL Server instance or to move databases from one instance of Windows Azure SQL Database to another. The deployment process is very straightforward. Only credentials associated with the Windows Azure SQL Database account are required; the wizard takes care of the rest.

- **Simplified cloud backup and cloud disaster recovery**   As mentioned earlier, SQL Server 2014 and Windows Azure are tightly integrated, providing organizations with the ability to implement hybrid scenarios such as backing up on-premises databases to the cloud. To achieve this goal, all that is required is a URL and a storage key. Then, a straightforward policy can be created and used to back up a single database or all databases within a SQL Server instance directly to Windows Azure storage. This process can be automatic or manual. Windows Azure storage provides additional benefits through out-of-the-box geo-replication. The use of geo-replication protects databases because the backups are stored in multiple Windows Azure data centers around the world, hence offering superior disaster recovery. Finally, the backups stored in Windows Azure can be restored on Windows Azure Virtual Machines (should a terrible disaster transpire, taking out an organization's on-premises data center).

- **Better together: AlwaysOn and Windows Azure**   Many organizations need to account for offsite disaster recovery, but they do not have a secondary data center or their secondary data center is within close proximity to the primary data center. Therefore, a single disaster could potentially take out both the primary and the secondary data centers, causing a major outage. In these cases, hybrid cloud provides organizations better disaster-recovery scenarios, and these scenarios also lower RTO (recovery time objective) and increase RPO (recovery point objective). As mentioned earlier, the Add Azure Replica wizard in SQL Server 2014 can be used to create secondary AlwaysOn asynchronous replicas in Windows Azure Virtual Machines. Therefore, in the event of a disaster, a replica can be failed over to the Windows Azure public cloud because all transactions committed on-premises will be sent asynchronously to the Windows Azure replica.

- **Extend on-premises applications**   An organization can take advantage of hybrid scenarios to extend and scale on-premises applications. For example, a physical retailer could use its on-premises SQL Server and supporting infrastructure to continue to serve physical retail transactions and utilize cloud-based Windows Azure infrastructure services to support online sales. Another scenario is a pizza organization that needs to scale to support the irregular peak demands of its business, which occur only on Super Bowl Sunday. The pizza maker could transition the web tier of its online pizza ordering system to Windows Azure while maintaining the back-end database on-premises. Windows Azure would provide the automatic scale-out functionality to support the irregular demand without the need to overprovision on-premises infrastructure, which would be costly and seldom used throughout the year.

- **Enhancing backups with Windows Azure Blob storage**   Windows Azure Blob storage allows for a flexible and reliable backup option that does not require the overhead of traditional hardware management, including the hassle and additional costs associated with storing backups offsite. In addition, by leveraging a direct backup to Windows Azure Blob storage, you can bypass the 16-disk limit, which was a concern in the past.

As you can see, SQL Server 2014 delivers many new capabilities for building hybrid-cloud solutions that use Microsoft's Cloud OS vision. This vision entails a consistent experience with a common set of tools across the entire application life cycle, no matter where you are running your data platform.

SQL Server 2014 editions

Similar to the previous version, SQL Server 2014 is available in three principal editions. All three editions have tighter alignment than their predecessors and were designed to meet the needs of almost any customer. Each edition comes in a 32-bit and 64-bit version. The principal editions, as shown in Figure 1-6, are the following:

- Enterprise edition

- Standard edition

- Business Intelligence edition

FIGURE 1-6 The main editions of SQL Server 2014.

Enterprise edition

The Enterprise edition of SQL Server 2014 is the uppermost SKU and is considered the premium offering. It is designed to meet the highest demands of large-scale data centers and data warehouse solutions by providing mission-critical performance and availability for tier 1 applications and the ability to deploy private-cloud, highly virtualized environments and large, centralized, or external-facing business-intelligence solutions.

Note The Datacenter edition included in the previous version of SQL Server is now retired. However, all capabilities of the Datacenter edition are in the Enterprise edition of SQL Server 2014.

The Enterprise edition features include the following:

- A maximum number of cores, subject to the operating system being used
- Unlimited virtualization
- AlwaysOn to achieve advanced high availability
- Unlimited virtualization for organizations with software assurance
- Support for the new columnstore indexing feature
- Advanced auditing
- Transparent data encryption
- Compression and partitioning

In addition, all the features and capabilities of the Business Intelligence edition are available, including:

- Reporting
- Analytics
- Multidimensional BI semantic model
- Data quality services
- Master data services
- In-memory tabular BI semantic model
- Self-service business intelligence

Standard edition

The Standard edition is a data-management platform tailored toward departmental databases and limited business-intelligence applications that are typically appropriate for medium-class solutions, smaller organizations, or departmental solutions. It does not include all the bells and whistles of the Enterprise and Business Intelligence editions, although it continues to offer best-in-class manageability and ease of use. Compared with the Enterprise and Business Intelligence editions, the Standard edition supports up to 16 cores and includes the following features:

- Spatial support

- FileTable

- Policy-based management

- Corporate business intelligence

- Reporting

- Analytics

- Multidimensional BI semantic model

- AlwaysOn 2-Node failover clustering to achieve basic high availability

- Up to four processors, up to 64 GB of RAM, one virtual machine, and two failover clustering nodes

Business Intelligence edition

The Business Intelligence edition offers organizations the full suite of powerful BI capabilities, such as scalable reporting and analytics, Power View, and PowerPivot. It is tailored toward organizations that need corporate business intelligence and self-service capabilities but do not require the full online transactional processing (OLTP) performance and scalability found in the Enterprise edition. Here is a high-level list of what the Business Intelligence edition includes:

- Up to a maximum of 16 cores for the Database Engine

- Maximum number of cores for business-intelligence processing

- All of the features found in the Standard edition

- Corporate business intelligence

  - Reporting

  - Analytics

  - Multidimensional BI semantic model

- Self-service capabilities

  - Alerting

  - Power View

  - PowerPivot for SharePoint Server

- Enterprise data management

  - Data quality services

  - Master data services

- In-memory tabular BI semantic model

- Basic high availability can be achieved with AlwaysOn 2-Node failover clustering

Specialized editions

Above and beyond the three principal editions of SQL Server 2014, Microsoft continues to deliver specialized editions for organizations that have a unique set of requirements. Some examples include the following:

- **Developer**   The Developer edition includes all the features and functionality found in the Enterprise edition; however, it is meant strictly for the purpose of development, testing, and demonstration. Note that you can transition a SQL Server Developer installation directly to production (without reinstallation) by upgrading it to SQL Server 2014 Enterprise.

- **Web**   Available at a much more affordable price than the Enterprise and Standard editions, the SQL Server 2014 Web edition is focused on service providers hosting Internet-facing web-services environments. Unlike the Express edition, this edition doesn't have database size restrictions, it supports four processors, and supports up to 64 GB of memory. SQL Server 2014 Web edition does not offer the same premium features found in the Enterprise and Standard editions, but it still remains the ideal platform for hosting websites and web applications.

- **Express**   This free edition is the best entry-level alternative for independent software vendors, nonprofessional developers, and hobbyists building client applications. Individuals learning about databases or learning how to build client applications will find that this edition meets all their needs. In a nutshell, this edition is limited to one processor and 1 GB of memory, and it can have a maximum database size of 10 GB. Also, Express is integrated with Microsoft Visual Studio.

> **Note**   To compare the different editions of SQL Server 2014 based on their key capabilities, review "Features Supported by the Editions of SQL Server 2014" at *http://msdn.microsoft. com/en-us/library/cc645993(v=sql.120).aspx* and *http://msdn.microsoft.com/en-us/library/ ms144275(v=sql.120).aspx*.

SQL Server 2014 licensing overview

The licensing models affiliated with SQL Server 2014 are simplified to better align to customer solutions and also optimized for virtualization and cloud deployments. Organizations should pay close attention to the information that follows to ensure that they understand the licensing model. With SQL Server 2014, the licensing for computing power is core-based and the Business Intelligence and Standard editions are available under the Server + Client Access License (CAL) model. In addition, organizations can save on cloud-based computing costs by licensing individual database virtual machines. Unfortunately, because each organization's environment is unique, this section cannot provide an overview of how the licensing changes affect an organization's environment. For more information on the licensing changes and how they influence your organization, please contact your Microsoft representative or partner. .

Hardware and software requirements

The recommended hardware and software requirements for SQL Server 2014 vary depending on the component being installed, the database workload, and the type of processor class that will be used. Review Table 1-1 and Table 1-2 to understand the hardware and software requirements for SQL Server 2014.

Because SQL Server 2014 supports many processor types and operating systems, Table 1-1 covers the hardware requirements only for a typical SQL Server 2014 installation. Typical installations include SQL Server 2014 Standard or Enterprise running on Windows Server 2012 R2 operating systems. Readers needing information for other scenarios should reference "Hardware and Software Requirements for Installing SQL Server 2014" at *http://msdn.microsoft.com/en-us/library/ms143506(v=SQL.120).aspx*.

TABLE 1-1 Hardware requirements

Hardware Component	Requirements
Processor	Processor type: (64-bit) x64 Minimum: AMD Opteron, AMD Athlon 64, Intel Xeon with Intel EM64T support, Intel Pentium IV with EM64T support Processor speed: minimum 1.4 GHz; 2.0 GHz or faster recommended Processor type: (32-bit) Intel Pentium III-compatible processor or faster Processor speed: minimum 1.0 GHz; 2.0 GHz or faster recommended
Memory (RAM)	Minimum: 1 GB Recommended: 4 GB or more Maximum: Operating system maximum
Disk Space	A minimum of 6 GB of available disk space; however, disk-space requirements will vary depending on the components you install. Database Engine: 811 MB Analysis Services: 345 MB Reporting Services: 304 MB Integration Services: 591 MB Client components: 1,823 MB

TABLE 1-2 Software requirements

Software Component	Requirements
Operating system	Windows Server 2012 R2 64-bit Datacenter, Enterprise, Standard, or Web edition; Windows Server 2012 64-bit Datacenter, Enterprise, Standard, or Web edition; or Windows Server 2008 R2 SP1 64-bit Datacenter, Enterprise, Standard, or Web edition.
.NET Framework	Microsoft .NET Framework 3.5 SP1 and Microsoft .NET Framework 4.0
Windows PowerShell	Windows PowerShell 2.0

Software Component	Requirements
SQL Server support tools and software	SQL Server 2014 - SQL Server Native Client SQL Server 2014 - SQL Server Setup Support Files Minimum: Windows Installer 4.5
Internet Explorer	Minimum: Windows Internet Explorer 7 or later version
Virtualization	Supported in virtual machine environments running on the Hyper-V role in Windows Server 2008 SP2 Standard, Enterprise, and Datacenter editions; Windows Server 2008 R2 SP1 Standard, Enterprise, and Datacenter editions; Windows Server 2012 Datacenter and Standard editions; Windows Server 2012 R2 Datacenter and Standard editions

Note The server hardware has supported both 32-bit and 64-bit processors for several years, but Windows Server 2008 R2 and above is 64-bit only. Take this into serious consideration when planning SQL Server 2014 deployments.

Installation, upgrade, and migration strategies

Like its predecessors, SQL Server 2014 is available in both 32-bit and 64-bit editions. Both can be installed either with the SQL Server installation wizard through a command prompt or with Sysprep for automated deployments with minimal administrator intervention. SQL Server 2014 supports installation on the Server Core, which is an installation option of Windows Server 2008 R2 SP1 or later. Finally, database administrators also have the option to upgrade an existing installation of SQL Server or conduct a side-by-side migration when installing SQL Server 2014. The following sections elaborate on the different strategies.

In-place upgrade

An in-place upgrade is the upgrade of an existing SQL Server installation to SQL Server 2014. When an in-place upgrade is conducted, the SQL Server 2014 setup program replaces the previous SQL Server binaries on the existing machine with the SQL Server 2014 binaries. SQL Server data is automatically converted from the previous version to SQL Server 2014. This means data does not have to be copied or migrated. In the example in Figure 1-7, a database administrator is conducting an in-place upgrade on a SQL Server 2012 instance running on Server 1. When the upgrade is complete, Server 1 still exists, but the SQL Server 2012 instance and all of its data is upgraded to SQL Server 2014.

Note Organizations can perform an in-place upgrade to SQL Server 2014 if they are running SQL Server 2008 SP3 or later, SQL Server 2008 R2 SP2 or later, or SQL Server 2012 SP1 or later. Unfortunately, earlier versions of SQL Server, including SQL Server 2005, SQL Server 2000, SQL Server 7.0, and SQL Server 6.5 cannot be upgraded to SQL Server 2014.

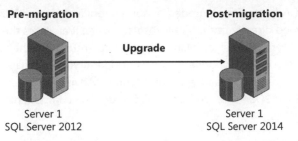

Pre-migration   Post-migration

Upgrade

Server 1
SQL Server 2012

Server 1
SQL Server 2014

FIGURE 1-7 An in-place upgrade from SQL Server 2012 to SQL Server 2014.

Review the information available through the following link for a detailed list of upgrades to SQL Server 2014 supported for earlier versions of SQL Server: *http://msdn.microsoft.com/en-us/library/ms143393(SQL.120).aspx*.

In-place upgrade pros and cons

The in-place upgrade strategy is usually easier and considered less risky than the side-by-side migration strategy. Upgrading is fairly fast, and additional hardware is not required. Because the names of the server and instances do not change during an upgrade process, applications still point to the old instances. As a result, this strategy is less time-consuming because no changes need to be made to application connection strings.

The disadvantage of an in-place upgrade is that it provides less granular control over the upgrade process. For example, when running multiple databases or components, a database administrator does not have the flexibility to choose individual items for upgrade. Instead, all databases and components are upgraded to SQL Server 2014 at the same time. In addition, the instance remains offline during the in-place upgrade, which means that if a mission-critical database or application or an important line-of-business application is running, a planned outage is required. Furthermore, if a disaster transpires during the upgrade, the rollback strategy can be a complex and time-consuming affair. A database administrator might have to install the operating system from scratch, install SQL Server, and then restore all the SQL Server data.

SQL Server 2014 high-level in-place strategy

The high-level in-place upgrade strategy for upgrading to SQL Server 2014 consists of the following steps:

1. Ensure that the instance of SQL Server to be upgraded meets the hardware and software requirements for SQL Server 2014.

2. Review the deprecated and discontinued features in SQL Server 2014. For more information, refer to "Deprecated Database Engine Features in SQL Server 2014" at *http://msdn.microsoft.com/en-us/library/ms143729(v=sql.120).aspx*.

3. Ensure that the version and edition of SQL Server that will be upgraded is supported. To review all the upgrade scenarios supported for SQL Server 2014, see "Supported Version and Edition Upgrades" at *http://msdn.microsoft.com/en-us/library/ms143393(v=sql.120).aspx*.

4. Run the SQL Server 2014 Upgrade Advisor. The Upgrade Advisor is a tool included with SQL Server 2014, or it can be downloaded directly from the Microsoft website. It analyzes the installed components on the SQL Server instance you plan to upgrade to ensure that the system supports SQL Server 2014. The Upgrade Advisor generates a report identifying anomalies that require fixing or attention before the upgrade can begin. The Upgrade Advisor analyzes any SQL Server 2012, SQL Server 2008 R2, SQL Server 2008, or SQL Server 2005 components that are installed.

5. Install the SQL Server 2014 prerequisites.

6. Begin the upgrade to SQL Server 2014 by running setup.

Side-by-side migration

The term *side-by-side migration* describes the deployment of a brand-new SQL Server 2014 instance alongside a legacy SQL Server instance. When the SQL Server 2014 installation is complete, a database administrator migrates data from the legacy SQL Server database platform to the new SQL Server 2014 database platform. Side-by-side migration is depicted in Figure 1-8.

Note You can conduct a side-by-side migration to SQL Server 2014 by using the same server. The side-by-side method can also be used to upgrade to SQL Server 2014 on a single server.

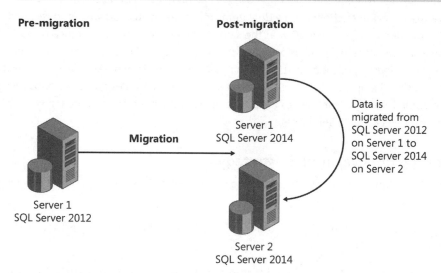

FIGURE 1-8 Side-by-side migration from SQL Server 2012 to SQL Server 2014.

Side-by-side migration pros and cons

The greatest advantage of a side-by-side migration over an in-place upgrade is the opportunity to build out a new database infrastructure on SQL Server 2014 and avoid potential migration issues that can occur with an in-place upgrade. A side-by-side migration also provides more granular control over the upgrade process because an administrator can migrate databases and components independently of one another. In addition, the legacy instance remains online during the migration process. All of these advantages result in a more powerful server. Moreover, when two instances are running in parallel, additional testing and verification can be conducted. Performing a rollback is also easy if a problem arises during the migration.

However, there are disadvantages to the side-by-side strategy. Additional hardware or a virtual machine may be required. Applications might also need to be directed to the new SQL Server 2014 instance, and it might not be a best practice for very large databases because of the duplicate amount of storage required during the migration process.

SQL Server 2014 high-level side-by-side strategy

The high-level side-by-side migration strategy for upgrading to SQL Server 2014 consists of the following steps:

1. Ensure that the instance of SQL Server you plan to migrate meets the hardware and software requirements for SQL Server 2014.

2. Review the deprecated and discontinued features in SQL Server 2014 by referring to "Deprecated Database Engine Features in SQL Server 2014" at *http://technet.microsoft.com/en-us/library/ms143729(v=sql.120).aspx*.

3. Although a legacy instance that is no longer supported will not be upgraded to SQL Server 2014, it is still beneficial to run the SQL Server 2014 Upgrade Advisor to ensure that the data being migrated to SQL Server 2014 is supported and there is no possibility of a blocker preventing the migration.

4. Procure the hardware and install your operating system of choice. Windows Server 2012 is recommended.

5. Install the SQL Server 2014 prerequisites and desired components.

6. Migrate objects from the legacy SQL Server to the new SQL Server 2014 database platform.

7. Point applications to the new SQL Server 2014 database platform.

8. Decommission legacy servers after the migration is complete.

CHAPTER 2

In-Memory OLTP investments

I n the previous two releases of SQL Server, Microsoft built into the product a number of in-memory capabilities to increase speed and throughput and to accelerate analytics. The first of these capabilities was an in-memory analytics add-in for Excel, also known as PowerPivot, in SQL Server 2008 R2. SQL Server 2012 included in-memory Analysis Services and in-memory columnstore. SQL Server 2014 comes with a new capability, known as In-Memory OLTP, designed to accelerate OLTP workloads. This feature, along with the other in-memory capabilities, provides organizations with a holistic approach to drive real-time business with real-time insights. This chapter focuses on the new capabilities associated with In-Memory OLTP.

In-Memory OLTP overview

Microsoft first announced work on the In-Memory OLTP feature during the 2012 PASS Summit in Seattle. For the worldwide database community, which has most likely known of this feature by its project name, Hekaton, the wait has now come to an end. Microsoft SQL Server 2014 includes this impressive new database engine feature that allows organizations to achieve significant performance gains for OLTP workloads while also reducing processing times. In many cases, when In-Memory OLTP is combined with new lock-free and latch-free algorithms that are optimized for accessing memory-resident data enhancements and natively compiled stored procedures, performance improved by up to 30 times.

To give database administrators the opportunity to appreciate this new feature, this chapter not only teaches and enlightens its readers, it also aims to dispel some flawed beliefs about In-Memory OLTP. This chapter addresses a series of questions, including the following:

- What are In-Memory OLTP and memory-optimized tables?

- How does In-Memory OLTP work?

- Are there real-world cases that demonstrate In-Memory OLTP performance gains?

- Can existing database applications be migrated to In-Memory OLTP?

Let's look under the hood to see how organizations can benefit from In-Memory OLTP.

The proliferation of data being captured across devices, applications, and services today has led organizations to work continuously on ways to lower the latency of applications while aiming to achieve maximum throughput of performance-critical data at a lower cost. Consider a financial organization that offers credit-card services to its customers. This organization must ensure that it can validate, authorize, and complete millions of transactions per second, or face the fact that it will lose financial opportunities for both itself and the vendors who use its service. Online gaming is another industry that requires maximum throughput, needing to service millions of customers who want to gamble online. Gone are the days when people made static bets on the outcome of a game. Today, people place bets in real time based on events transpiring in real time. Take, for example, a football game for which your bet depends on whether you believe the kicker will kick the winning field goal in the Super Bowl. In situations like this, the database platform must be well equipped to process millions of transactions concurrently at low latency, or the online gaming organization faces the possibility that it could experience financial ruin.

The SQL Server product group recognized that customer requirements were quickly changing in the data world and that the group needed to provide new capabilities to decrease processing times and deliver higher throughput at lower latency. Fortunately, the world was also experiencing a steady trend in the hardware industry that allowed the product group to generate these new capabilities. First, the product group realized that the cost of memory had vastly decreased over the past 20 to 25 years, while the size of memory continued to increase. Moreover, the cost of memory had reached a price point and a capacity point at which it was now viable to have large amounts of data in memory. This trend is illustrated in Figure 2-1.

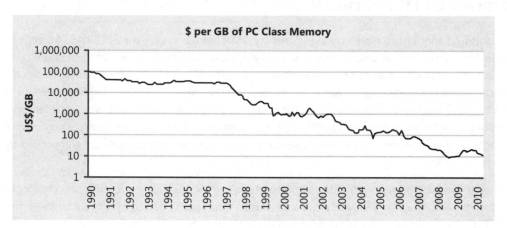

FIGURE 2-1 The price of RAM has drastically decreased over the past 20 years.

Second, the group recognized both that CPU clock rates had plateaued and that CPU clock rates were not getting any faster even after the number of cores on a processor had drastically increased, as shown in Figure 2-2. Armed with knowledge from these trends, the SQL Server team reevaluated the way SQL Server processes data from disk and designed the new In-Memory OLTP engine, which can take full advantage of the larger memory sizes that are available and use processors with more cores to significantly improve performance of OLTP applications.

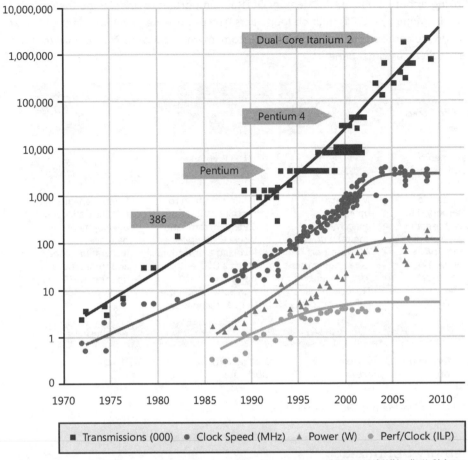

Intel CPU Trends*

*sources: Intel, Wikipedia, K. Olukotun

FIGURE 2-2 Stagnating growth in CPU clock speeds while the number of cores increase.

On average, most OLTP databases are 1 terabyte or less. As such, the majority of today's production OLTP databases can reap the performance benefits of In-Memory OLTP because the whole database can fit into memory. Just imagine the possibilities should the current hardware trend continue. Perhaps in the next decade, servers will support petabytes of memory, making it possible to move the largest databases and workloads to memory. It will be interesting to see what the future holds.

In-Memory OLTP fundamentals and architecture

The next few sections discuss In-Memory OLTP fundamentals, architecture, concepts, terminology, hardware and software requirements, and some myths about how it is implemented in SQL Server 2014.

Four In-Memory OLTP architecture pillars

Before thinking about how to use In-Memory OLTP, it is important to understand the underlying architecture. In-Memory OLTP is built on four pillars. The pillars were developed in the context of industry hardware and business trends to offer customer benefits. Figure 2-3 summarizes the four pillars and associated customer benefits.

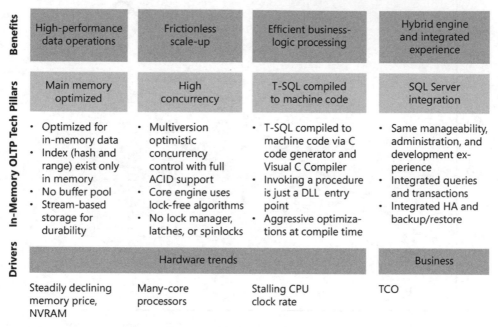

	High-performance data operations	Frictionless scale-up	Efficient business-logic processing	Hybrid engine and integrated experience
Benefits				
In-Memory OLTP Tech Pillars	Main memory optimized	High concurrency	T-SQL compiled to machine code	SQL Server integration
	• Optimized for in-memory data • Index (hash and range) exist only in memory • No buffer pool • Stream-based storage for durability	• Multiversion optimistic concurrency control with full ACID support • Core engine uses lock-free algorithms • No lock manager, latches, or spinlocks	• T-SQL compiled to machine code via C code generator and Visual C Compiler • Invoking a procedure is just a DLL entry point • Aggressive optimizations at compile time	• Same manageability, administration, and development experience • Integrated queries and transactions • Integrated HA and backup/restore
Drivers	Hardware trends			Business
	Steadily declining memory price, NVRAM	Many-core processors	Stalling CPU clock rate	TCO

FIGURE 2-3 Pillars of In-Memory OLTP architecture.

Main memory optimized

As a result of the steady decline in the price of memory and the rapid rate at which the size of memory was growing, putting tables in main memory became feasible, thereby replacing the need to place and access tables on disk. With this change came a significant reduction in the time required to gain access to tables, because pages were no longer required to be read into cache from disk. New functionality, such as hash indexes and nonclustered range indexes, can exploit data that is in physical memory rather than on disk, which allows for faster access and higher performance in data operations.

T-SQL compiled to machine code

The SQL Server product group recognized that if it could reduce the number of instructions needed to execute the same logic, it could do the same work and also decrease processing time. The product group implemented this idea by transforming SQL stored procedures to a C program and then compiling the program into a DLL by using the Visual C compiler. The resulting machine code replaced stored procedures and the usual interpretation of logic through query execution. This made it possible to run a stored procedure by using fewer instructions, leading to more efficient business-logic processing that was significantly faster. With the optimization in processing time, internal testing at the lower level of the storage engine verified that machine code could reduce the instruction count by 30 to 50 times, which resulted in a proportional increase in throughput and in lower latency.

High concurrency

SQL Server has scaled extremely well because of the performance and scalability improvements made over the past releases. Unfortunately, certain application patterns—for example, a last page insert in the clustering key order or concurrent updates of hot pages—still suffered latch contention and did not scale as well as a result. The additional improvements implemented through In-Memory OLTP in SQL Server 2014 allow for higher concurrency. First, the product group did away with page structures for accessing memory-optimized tables. This means that no paging or latching occurs to create bottlenecks. Second, the core engine uses lock-free algorithm structures that are based on multiversion optimistic concurrency control with full ACID (atomic, consistent, isolated, and durable) support. These improvements remove common scalability bottlenecks and provide high concurrency and frictionless scale-up opportunities to increase overall performance when memory–optimized tables are used.

SQL Server integration

The SQL Server product group decided that In-Memory OLTP should be easy to consume and that performance-critical tables should take advantage of this feature. What evolved from this idea is an In-Memory OLTP engine that is fully integrated into the SQL Server Database Engine and managed with a familiar set of tools. People who are familiar with SQL Server can quickly make use of the benefits of In-Memory OLTP because the management, administration, and development experiences are the same. Moreover, In-Memory OLTP works seamlessly with other features, such as AlwaysOn Availability Groups, AlwaysOn Failover Cluster Instances, replication, backups, and restores.

In-Memory OLTP concepts and terminology

The following section reviews In-Memory OLTP concepts and terminology:

- **Disk-based tables**   This is the traditional way SQL Server has stored data since the product's inception. Data in a table is stored in 8-KB pages and read and written to disk. Each table also had its own data and index pages.

- **Memory-optimized tables**   Memory-optimized tables are the alternative to traditional disk-based tables and follow the new structures associated with In-Memory OLTP. The primary store for memory-optimized tables is main memory, but a second copy in a different format is maintained on disk for durability purposes.

- **Native compilation**   To achieve faster data access and efficient query execution, SQL Server natively compiles stored procedures that access memory-optimized tables into native DLLs. When stored procedures are natively compiled, the need for additional compilation and interpretation is reduced. Also, compilation provides additional performance enhancements, as compared with using memory-optimized tables alone.

- **Interop**   In this process, interpreted Transact-SQL batches and stored procedures are used instead of a natively compiled stored procedure when accessing data in a memory-optimized table. Interop is used to simplify application migration.

- **Cross-container transactions**   This is a hybrid approach in which transactions use both memory-optimized tables and disk-based tables.

- **Durable and nondurable tables**   By default, memory-optimized tables are completely durable and offer full ACID support. Note that memory-optimized tables that are not durable are still supported by SQL Server, but the contents of a table exist only in memory and are lost when the server restarts. The syntax DURABILITY=SCHEMA_ONLY is used to create nondurable tables.

Hardware and software requirements for memory-optimized tables

A unified experience for organizations has been created in every area—including but not limited to deployment and support—through the tight integration of In-Memory OLTP with SQL Server 2014. However, before you try this new capability, you should become acquainted with the requirements for using memory-optimized tables. In addition to the general hardware and software requirements for installing SQL Server 2014 (described in Chapter 1, "SQL Server 2014 editions and engine enhancements"), here are the requirements for using memory-optimized tables:

- Production environments require the 64-bit Enterprise edition of SQL Server 2014 with the Database Engine Services component. The Developer edition can also be used when developing and testing. The 32-bit environments are not supported.

- To store data in tables and also in indexes, SQL Server requires sufficient memory. You must configure memory to accommodate memory-optimized tables and to have indexes be fully resident in memory.

- When configuring memory for SQL Server, you should account for the size of the buffer pool needed for the disk-based tables and for other internal structures.

- The processor used for the instance of SQL Server must support the cmpxchg16b instruction.

In-Memory OLTP use cases

Many use cases show the benefits of In-Memory OLTP. Consider these scenarios:

- An application that is incurring high latch contention can alleviate this contention and scale up by converting tables from disk-based tables to memory-optimized tables.

- Natively compiled stored procedures can be used to address low-latency scenarios because In-Memory OLTP reduces the response times associated with poor performing procedures (assuming that business logic can be compiled).

- Many scale-out operations that require only read access suffer from CPU performance bottle-necks. By moving the data to In-Memory OLTP, it is possible to significantly reduce CPU. With higher scalability, this allows you to take advantage of existing processing resources to achieve higher throughput.

- Think about the data-staging and load phases of a typical ETL process. At times, numerous operations need to be completed, including gathering data from an outside source and uploading it to a staging table in SQL Server, making changes to the data, and then transferring the data to a target table. For these types of operations, nondurable memory-optimized tables provide an efficient way to store staging data by completely eliminating storage cost, including transactional logging.

Myths about In-Memory OLTP

Before moving on to the next section and walking through some In-Memory OLTP examples, it's useful to rectify some of the misconceptions surrounding In-Memory OLTP.

- **Myth 1: SQL Server In-Memory OLTP is a recent response to competitors' offerings** Work on In-Memory OLTP commenced approximately four years ago in response to business and hardware trends occurring in the industry.

- **Myth 2: In-Memory OLTP is like DBCC PINTABLE** DBCC PINTABLE was an old operation in SQL Server 7 that made it possible for the pages associated with a table to be read into the buffer pool and remain in memory instead of being removed or deleted. Although there are some similarities, In-Memory OLTP is a new design focused on optimizing in-memory data operations. There are no pages or buffer pool for memory-optimized tables.

- **Myth 3: In-memory databases are new separate products** Unlike with many of its competitors, In-Memory OLTP is fully integrated into SQL Server 2014. If you know SQL Server, you know In-Memory OLTP.

- **Myth 4: You can use In-Memory OLTP in an existing SQL Server application without any changes** In reality, a few changes are required. At the very least, some changes to the schema will need to be made.

- **Myth 5: Since tables are in memory, the data is not durable or highly available—I will lose it after a server crash** In reality, In-Memory OLTP is fully durable and includes several highly available features, including AlwaysOn features. Data is persisted on disk and will survive a server crash.

In-Memory OLTP integration and application migration

A before-and-after illustration is the best way to compare the internal behavior of SQL Server when transactions are processed using traditional disk-based tables as opposed to memory-optimized tables. Figure 2-4 shows how a traditional transaction from a client application is processed using disk-based tables. Figure 2-6, shown later in the chapter, demonstrates the processing behavior when the same tables are migrated to memory-optimized tables and the In-Memory OLTP engine is used. Both figures also illustrate how tightly coupled In-Memory OLTP is with the Database Engine component.

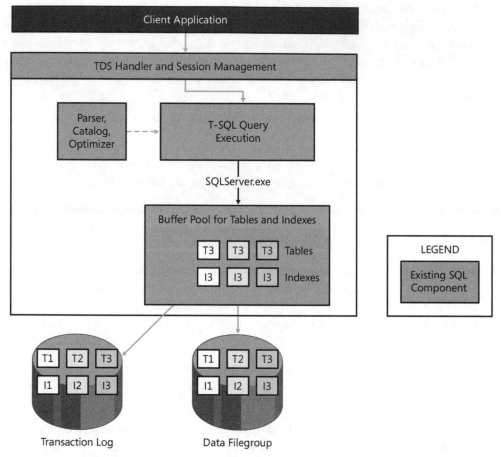

FIGURE 2-4 Client application process using disk-based table access.

In Figure 2-4, the SQL Server Database Engine communicates with the client application by using a Microsoft communication format called a Tabular Data Stream (TDS). The transaction goes through a parser and a catalog and an optimizer, and the T-SQL query is compiled for execution. During execution, the data is fetched from storage into the buffer pool for changes. At the time the transaction is committed, the log records are flushed to disk. The changes to the data and index pages are flushed to disk asynchronously.

Will In-Memory OLTP improve performance?

Figure 2-4 depicts a traditional scenario using disk-based tables. Although the processing times are sufficient in this example, it is not hard to conceive that further optimization of the database application's performance will be needed one day. When that day comes, organizations can use the native tools in SQL Server to help them determine whether In-Memory OLTP is right for their environment. Specifically, organizations can use the Analysis, Migrate and Report (AMR) tool built into SQL Server Management Studio. The following steps can determine whether In-Memory OLTP is right for an organization:

1. Establish a system performance baseline.

2. Configure the Management Data Warehouse (MDW).

3. Configure data collection.

4. Run a workload.

5. Run the AMR tool.

6. Analyze results from AMR reports and migrate tables.

7. Migrate stored procedures.

8. Run workload again and collect performance metrics.

9. Compare new workload performance results to the original baseline.

10. Complete.

Ultimately, the AMR tool analyzes the workload to determine whether In-Memory OLTP will improve performance. It also helps organizations plan and execute their migration to memory-optimized tables. In addition, the report provides scan statistics, contention statistics, execution statistics, table references, and migration issues to ensure that organizations are given a wealth of information to further assist them with their analysis and eventually their migration.

Using the Memory Optimization Advisor to migrate disk-based tables

After running the AMR tool and identifying a table to port to In-Memory OLTP, you can use the Table Memory Optimization Advisor to help migrate specific disk-based tables to memory-optimized tables. Do this by right-clicking a table in Management Studio and then selecting Memory Optimization Advisor. This step invokes a wizard that begins conducting validation tests and providing migration warnings, as illustrated in Figure 2-5. The wizard also requires users to make a number of decisions about memory optimization, such as selecting which memory-optimized filegroup to use, the logical file name, and the file path. Finally, the wizard allows users to rename the original table, estimates current memory cost in megabytes, and prompts users to specify whether to use data durability for copying table data to the new memory-optimized table.

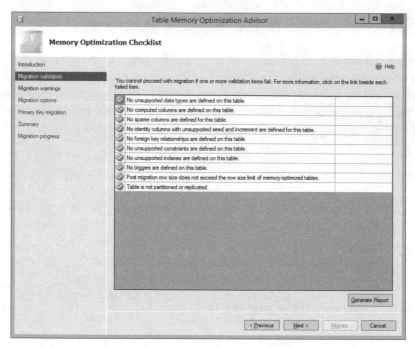

FIGURE 2-5 Using the Table Memory Optimization Advisor checklist to migrate disk-based tables.

Analyzing In-Memory OLTP behavior after memory-optimized table migration

Now it's time to take account of Figure 2-6. Let's assume that the AMR tool made a recommendation to migrate Tables 1 and 2 in the example depicted in Figure 2-4 to memory-optimized tables. Figure 2-6 focuses on In-Memory OLTP behavior after migration to memory-optimized tables has occurred and stored procedures have been natively compiled.

A new area of memory is added for memory-optimized tables and indexes. In addition, a full suite of new DMVs, XEvents, and instrumentation is also added, allowing the engine to keep track of memory utilization. Finally, a memory-optimized filegroup, which is based on the semantics of FILESTREAM, is also added. Access to memory-optimized tables can occur via query interop, natively compiled stored procedures, or a hybrid approach. In addition, indexes for In-Memory OLTP are not persisted. They reside only in memory and are loaded when the database is started or is brought online.

Query interop is the easiest way to migrate the application to In-Memory OLTP and access memory-optimized tables. This method does not use native compilations. It uses either ad hoc inter-preted Transact-SQL or traditional stored procedures, which is the approach depicted by option 1 in Figure 2-6. As an alternative, natively compiled stored procedures are the fastest way to access data in memory-optimized tables. This approach is depicted by option 2 in Figure 2-6.

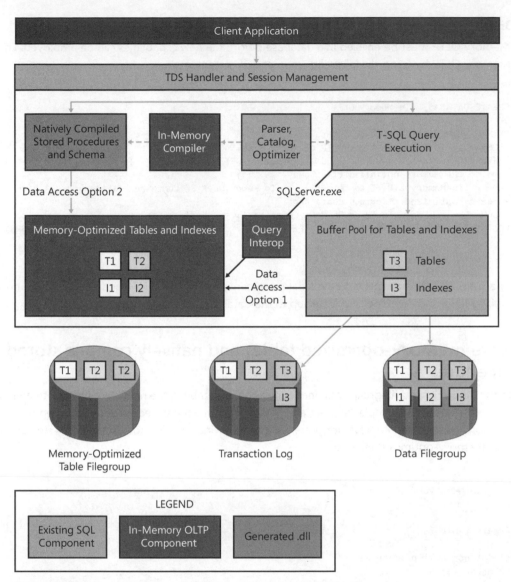

FIGURE 2-6 Client application process based on memory-optimized table access.

Using In-Memory OLTP

The following examples outline how to use In-Memory OLTP and memory-optimized tables to improve performance of OLTP applications through efficient, memory-optimized data access and native compilation of business logic.

Enabling In-Memory OLTP in a database

In-Memory OLTP must be enabled in a database before the new capabilities can be employed. Enable In-Memory OLTP by using the following Transact-SQL statements:

```
CREATE DATABASE [In-MemoryOLTP]
ON
PRIMARY(NAME = [In-MemoryOLTP_data],
FILENAME = 'c:\data\In-MemoryOLTP_db.mdf', size=500MB)
, FILEGROUP [In-MemoryOLTP_db] CONTAINS MEMORY_OPTIMIZED_DATA( -- In-MemoryOLTP_db is the
name of the memory-optimized filegroup
NAME = [In-MemoryOLTP_FG_Container],   -- In-MemoryOLTP_FG_Container is the logical name of
a memory-optimized filegroup container
FILENAME = 'c:\data\In-MemoryOLTP_FG_Container') -- physical path to the container
LOG ON (name = [In-MemoryOLTP_log], Filename='C:\data\In-MemoryOLTP_log.ldf', size=500MB)
GO
```

The Transact-SQL statements create a database named In-MemoryOLTP and also add a memory-optimized filegroup container and filegroup to the database.

Create memory-optimized tables and natively compile stored procedures

With the filegroup and filegroup container added to the database, the next step is to create memory-optimized tables in the sample database and natively compile the stored procedures to reduce the instructions needed and improve performance. The following sample code executes this step and also creates memory-optimized indexes:

```
use [In-MemoryOLTP]
go

create table [sql]
(
c1 int not null primary key,
c2 nchar(48) not null
)
go
create table [hash]
(
c1 int not null primary key nonclustered hash with (bucket_count=1000000),
c2 nchar(48) not null
) with (memory_optimized=on, durability = schema_only)
go
create table [hash1]
(
c1 int not null primary key nonclustered hash with (bucket_count=1000000),
c2 nchar(48) not null
) with (memory_optimized=on, durability = schema_only)
go
```

```
CREATE PROCEDURE yy
       @rowcount int,
       @c nchar(48)
WITH NATIVE_COMPILATION, SCHEMABINDING, EXECUTE AS OWNER
AS
 BEGIN ATOMIC
 WITH (TRANSACTION ISOLATION LEVEL = SNAPSHOT, LANGUAGE = N'us_english')
       declare @i int = 1
       while @i <= @rowcount
       begin
               INSERT INTO [dbo].[hash1] values (@i, @c)
               set @i += 1
       end
END
GO
```

Execute queries to demonstrate performance when using memory-optimized tables

Now that the database, memory-optimized tables, and stored procedures are created, it's time to evaluate the performance gains by executing the following scripts and comparing the processing times of the disk-based table and interpreted Transact-SQL, the memory-optimized table with the hash index and interpreted Transact-SQL, and the memory-optimized table with the hash index and a natively compiled stored procedure.

```
set statistics time off
set nocount on
-- inserts - 1 at a time
declare @starttime datetime2 = sysdatetime(),
       @timems int
declare @i int = 1
declare @rowcount int = 100000
declare @c nchar(48) = N'123456789012345678901234567890012345678'
-----------------------------
--- disk-based table and interpreted Transact-SQL
-----------------------------
begin tran
while @i <= @rowcount
begin
       insert into [sql] values (@i, @c)
       set @i += 1
end
commit
set @timems = datediff(ms, @starttime, sysdatetime())
select 'Disk-based table and interpreted Transact-SQL: ' + cast(@timems as varchar(10)) +
' ms'
-----------------------------
--- Interop Hash
-----------------------------
set @i = 1
```

```
set @starttime = sysdatetime()
begin tran
while @i <= @rowcount
begin
        insert into [hash] values (@i, @c)
        set @i += 1
end
commit
set @timems = datediff(ms, @starttime, sysdatetime())
select ' memory-optimized table with hash index and interpreted Transact-SQL: ' + cast(@
timems as varchar(10)) + ' ms'
----------------------------
--- Compiled Hash
----------------------------
set @starttime = sysdatetime()
exec yy @rowcount, @c
set @timems = datediff(ms, @starttime, sysdatetime())
select 'memory-optimized table with hash index and native Stored Procedure:' + cast(@
timems as varchar(10)) + ' ms'
```

The processing times are illustrated in the results window of SQL Server Management Studio. Using commodity hardware such as eight virtual processors and 14 GB of RAM, the processing time of the disk-based table and interpreted Transact-SQL was 3,219ms. The memory-optimized table with a hash index and interpreted Transact-SQL took 1015ms, and the memory-optimized table with a hash index and natively compiled stored procedure took 94ms. This clearly demonstrates a significantly faster processing time—approximately 34 times faster.

Appendix

Memory-optimized table

```
CREATE TABLE
    [ database_name . [ schema_name ] . | schema_name . ]
    table_name
        ( { <column_definition>
        | [ <table_constraint> ] [ ,...n ]
        | [ <table_index> ] [ ,...n ]
        } )
        [ WITH ( <table_option> [ ,...n ] ) ]
        [ ; ]
<column_definition> ::=
column_name <data_type>
    [ COLLATE collation_name ]
    NOT NULL
    [ <column_constraint> ]
    [ <column_index> ]
<data type> ::=
[ type_schema_name . ] type_name [ ( precision [ , scale ]) ]
```

```
<column_constraint> ::=
    [ CONSTRAINT constraint_name ]
    { PRIMARY KEY NONCLUSTERED HASH WITH (BUCKET_COUNT
    = <bucket_count>) }

< table_constraint > ::=
    [ CONSTRAINT constraint_name ]
    { PRIMARY KEY NONCLUSTERED HASH (column [ ,...n ] )
    WITH (BUCKET_COUNT = <bucket_count>) }
 <column_index> ::=
    [ INDEX index_name ]
    { HASH WITH (BUCKET_COUNT = <bucket_count>) }
<table_index> ::=
    [ INDEX index_name ]
    [ INDEX constraint_name ]
    { HASH (column [ ,...n ] ) WITH (BUCKET_COUNT
    = <bucket_count>) }
<table_option> ::=
{
    [MEMORY_OPTIMIZED = {ON | OFF}]
    | [DURABILITY = {SCHEMA_ONLY | SCHEMA_AND_DATA}]
}
```

Natively compiled stored procedure

```
CREATE { PROC | PROCEDURE } [schema_name.] procedure_name
    [ { @parameter data_type } [ = default ] [ OUT | OUTPUT ]
[READONLY]] ] [ ,...n ]
[ WITH <procedure_option> [ ,...n ] ]
AS
{
    [ BEGIN [ATOMIC WITH ( <set_option> [ ,...n ] ) ] ]
    sql_statement [;] [ ...n ]
    [ END ]
}
[;]
<procedure_option> ::=
    | EXECUTE AS clause
    | NATIVE_COMPILATION
    | SCHEMABINDING

<set_option> ::=
    LANGUAGE = [ N ] 'language'
    | TRANSACTION ISOLATION LEVEL = { REPEATABLE READ | SERIALIZABLE | SNAPSHOT }
        [ | DATEFIRST = number
            | DATEFORMAT = format ]

<sql_statement>:

 -DECLARE variable
-SET -IF/WHILE -TRY/CATCH/THROW -RETURN
```

```
-SELECT [TOP <n>] <column_list>
FROM <table>
    [WHERE <predicate>]
    [ORDER BY <expression_list>]
INSERT <table> [(<column_list>)] VALUES (<value_list>)
INSERT <table> [(<column_list>)] SELECT …
UPDATE <table> SET <assignment_list> [WHERE <predicate>]
DELETE <table> [WHERE <predicate>]
```

High-availability, hybrid-cloud, and backup enhancements

M icrosoft SQL Server 2014 delivers significant enhancements to well-known critical capabilities
such as high availability and disaster recovery and provides an integrated hybrid-cloud platform. These enhancements promise to assist organizations in achieving their highest level of confidence to date in their data platform environments and offer new innovative solutions and business
models via the cloud.

This chapter aims to bring readers up to date on the high-availability, hybrid-cloud, and backup
capabilities that are fully integrated into SQL Server 2014 and Windows Azure. In addition, this chapter showcases how the cloud is rapidly changing the world of information technology and the way organizations innovate and do business, which may one day render many of the traditional approaches
and methodologies used today obsolete.

Figure 3-1 illustrates the Microsoft Cloud OS vision, which allows organizations to achieve the benefits of scale, speed, and agility while protecting existing investments. This means that organizations
can rapidly build and deploy database applications and support real-time analytics across all forms of
data with a consistent experience, whether on-premises, off-premises, or through hybrid-cloud solutions.

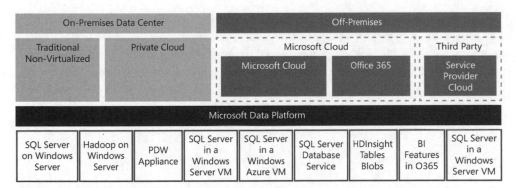

FIGURE 3-1 The elements of the Microsoft Cloud OS vision as they relate to the Microsoft data platform to
achieve a consistent experience on-premises, off-premises, or on hybrid-cloud solutions.

We'll focus first on the high-availability and disaster-recovery enhancements, specifically AlwaysOn Availability Groups and AlwaysOn Failover Cluster Instances. The chapter then showcases hybrid-cloud solutions with Windows Azure and backup enhancements.

SQL Server high-availability and disaster-recovery enhancements

Every organization's success and service reputation is built on ensuring that its data is always accessible and protected. In the IT world, this means delivering a product that achieves the highest level of availability and disaster recovery while simultaneously minimizing data loss and downtime. In SQL Server 2012, Microsoft introduced a new capability known as AlwaysOn, which provided customers superior availability and disaster-recovery alternatives. The AlwaysOn brand included two features for achieving high availability and disaster recovery: AlwaysOn Availability Groups and AlwaysOn Failover Cluster Instances (FCIs). The next few sections discuss the AlwaysOn enhancements in SQL Server 2014.

AlwaysOn Availability Groups enhancements

AlwaysOn Availability Groups gave organizations the ability to automatically or manually fail over a group of databases as a single unit with support for up to four secondary replicas. The solution was integrated with SQL Server Management Studio and provided high availability and disaster recovery with zero data loss. It could be deployed on local storage or shared storage, and it supported both synchronous and asynchronous data movement. The application failover was very fast and supported automatic page repair, and the secondary replicas could be used to offload reporting and a number of maintenance tasks such as backups. Figure 3-2 depicts an AlwaysOn Availability Groups deployment strategy that is based on SQL Server 2012. The illustration shows one primary replica and three secondary replicas.

AlwaysOn Availability Groups was a great success, yet the SQL Server product group wanted to expand its capabilities and provide increased availability, greater efficiency, and easier deployment and management. Similarly, the product group wanted to provide tighter integration with Windows Azure for hybrid-cloud opportunities and innovations. The next sections explore the results of the product group's efforts.

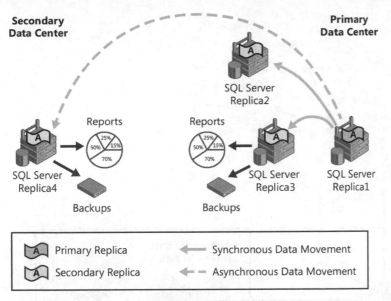

FIGURE 3-2 An AlwaysOn Availability Groups deployment running SQL Server 2012 with four replicas spanning two data centers for high availability and disaster recovery.

Additional secondary replicas

To provide additional offloading capabilities, the maximum number of secondary replicas was increased from four to eight in SQL Server 2014. Some readers may ask why more replicas were needed. Additional replicas can be distributed around the world, which positively affects high availability and disaster-recovery efforts for any organization. New wizards have also been included that can be used to provide integrated hybrid-cloud scenarios in which replicas can be easily deployed in Windows Azure. Likewise, additional replicas can also be used to offload read workloads such as scale-out operations, reporting backups, and maintenance tasks. It is worth keeping in mind that eight secondaries, two of which can be configured as synchronous secondaries, can be used for high availability.

Figure 3-3 illustrates an AlwaysOn Availability Groups deployment with SQL Server 2014. Here, the deployment uses a primary replica and seven secondary replicas. The secondary replicas provide maximum high availability and disaster-recovery protection because they reside in the primary data center, the secondary data center, and in the Windows Azure cloud.

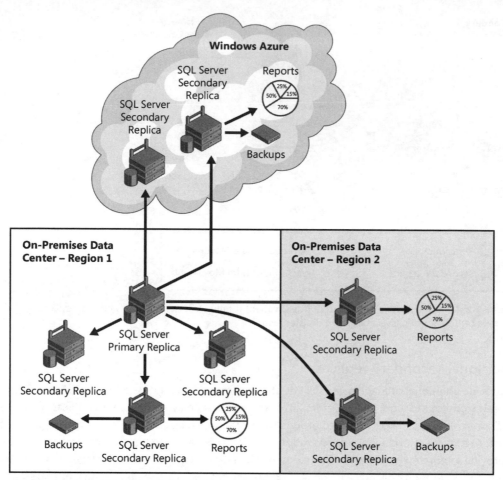

FIGURE 3-3 An AlwaysOn Availability Groups deployment running SQL Server 2014 with a total of eight replicas. Two of these replicas reside in Windows Azure to provide disaster-recovery capabilities in the cloud.

Increased availability

In SQL Server 2012, read workloads on a secondary replica failed if a network failure occurred between the primary replica and the secondary replicas. This type of situation arose more often in geo-distributed environments or hybrid deployments because of their increased susceptibility to network equipment failures, network upgrades, or ISP failures. With SQL Server 2014, the availability of readable secondary replicas has been increased and read workloads are no longer affected during network failures, if the primary is down or if the cluster quorum is lost. To make use of this enhancement, a direct connection to a readable secondary is required. In addition, as indicated earlier, whether initiated manually or automatically, a failover of multiple databases can occur concurrently, leading to higher availability. Figure 3-4 details the benefits of increased availability in SQL Server 2014. In the figure, two secondary replicas are used for reporting and backups even though the network connection to the primary is no longer available.

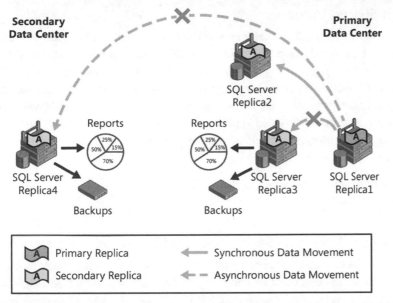

FIGURE 3-4 Increased availability and functionality of secondary replicas with SQL Server 2014.

Add Azure Replica wizard

Disaster-recovery and business-continuity planning are important requirements for many organizations, both from a customer-service and a regulatory perspective. Data loss and system disasters can negatively impact an organization or even permanently shut it down. Hence, the need for disaster-recovery sites. Regrettably, many organizations still do not have a disaster-recovery site because of the high costs and maintenance challenges. To address these challenges, SQL Server 2012 supported secondary replicas on Windows Azure Virtual Machines. This meant that organizations could manage disaster recovery by building hybrid platforms using Microsoft's cloud platform, known as Windows Azure. Organizations indicated that this opportunity addressed their disaster-recovery requirements, but it also created another issue. The configuration process for database administrators was manual and cumbersome at times. The product group responded to the feedback and has introduced the Add Azure Replica wizard in SQL Server 2014. The wizard automates and simplifies the deployment of on-premises replicas to Windows Azure. When configuring the replicas, a database administrator can choose any Windows Azure data center around the world; however, when a location is considered primarily in terms of latency and politics, the best location for the replicas is near the data center.

AlwaysOn Failover Cluster Instances enhancements

Now that we've explored the development efforts in engineering the new capabilities of AlwaysOn Availability Groups for high availability and disaster recovery, it's time to move on to another important matter: enhancements to AlwaysOn Failover Cluster Instances (FCIs).

Support for Cluster Shared Volumes

In conjunction with Windows Server 2012 and later releases, SQL Server 2014 now supports Cluster Shared Volumes (CSVs) as clustered shared disks for AlwaysOn Failover Cluster Instances. Why is this important? CSVs reduce the number of logical unit numbers (LUNs), or disks, required for FCIs, which increases the number of FCIs that can be hosted on a single Windows Server Failover Cluster (WSFC). Previously, the maximum number of instances supported was 24 because a LUN was the unit of failover. CSVs remove this limitation. CSVs also improve storage area network (SAN) utilization and disk space and increase I/O resiliency and failover resiliency because disks no longer need to be unmounted and mounted.

The following sections outline how to add a CSV on a Windows Server Failover Cluster and how to use it during a SQL Server installation.

Add a disk to a CSV on a Windows Server Failover Cluster

In Windows Server 2012 R2, the CSV feature is enabled by default when the failover cluster feature is installed. To add a disk to a CSV, the disk must be added to the Available Storage group of the cluster before it is added to the CSV on the cluster. You can use Failover Cluster Manager or the Failover Clustering cmdlets in Windows PowerShell to perform these procedures.

To add a disk to the Available Storage group, follow these steps:

1. In the console tree in Failover Cluster Manager, expand the name of the cluster, and then expand Storage.

2. Right-click Disks, and then click Add Disk. A list appears showing the disks that can be added for use in a failover cluster.

3. Select the disk or disks you want to add, and then click OK.

The next steps add the disk or disks in the Availability Storage group to the CSV:

1. In the console tree in Failover Cluster Manager, expand the name of the cluster, expand Storage, and then click Disks.

2. Select one or more disks that are assigned to Available Storage, right-click the selection, and then click Add To Cluster Shared Volumes.

The disks are now assigned to the Cluster Shared Volume group in the cluster. The disks are exposed to each cluster node as numbered volumes (mount points) under the %SystemDisk%ClusterStorage folder. The volumes appear in the CSVFS file system.

Figure 3-5 shows two 100-GB CSVs (named Cluster Disk 2-CSV1 and Cluster Disk 3-CSV2) that have been allocated to a Windows Server Failover Cluster named AlwaysOn-FC01.

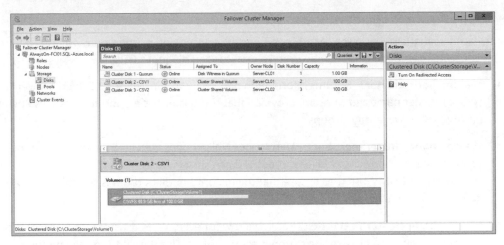

FIGURE 3-5 Adding available storage to Cluster Shared Volumes in Failover Cluster Manager.

The next step is installing the SQL Server failover cluster instance and leveraging the CSVs. Launch SQL Server setup and choose New SQL Server Failover Cluster Installation to invoke the Install A SQL Server Failover Cluster wizard. When you get to the Cluster Disk Selection page, select the Cluster Shared Volume to use as the shared cluster disk resources for your SQL Server failover cluster. As illustrated in Figure 3-6, Cluster Disk 2-CSV1, which was created in the preceding procedure, is used as the CSV on which to install the FCI.

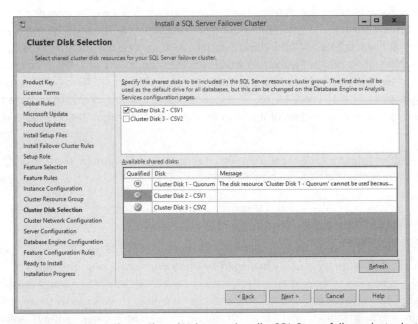

FIGURE 3-6 Using a Cluster Shared Volume to install a SQL Server failover cluster instance.

New dynamic management views (DMVs)

New dynamic management views (DMVs) have been introduced and existing ones optimized to return server state information that can be used to monitor and diagnose FCIs:

- **sys.dm_hadr_cluster**   Returns information pertaining to the Windows Server Failover Cluster (WSFC) cluster name and quorum, provided that the cluster has a quorum. It can also be used on AlwaysOn Availability Groups.

- **sys.dm_hadr_cluster_members**   Determines which nodes are currently running on the WSFC cluster and how many failures the WSFC can sustain before losing a quorum. This is a very important DMV. Use it to ensure that the majority-node quorum is set up correctly to guard against unexpected failure.

- **sys.dm_hadr_cluster_networks**   Returns a row for every WSFC cluster member that is participating in an availability group's subnet configuration. Use this DMV to validate the network virtual IP that is configured for each availability replica.

- **sys.dm_io_cluster_valid_path_names**   A new DMV used to return information on all valid shared disks, including CSVs.

Platform for hybrid cloud

SQL Server 2014 is meeting the increasing demands of organizations to reduce operation and hardware costs, provide high availability, and scale their businesses (among other requests) by offering a hybrid-cloud environment with tailored hybrid-cloud solutions such as backing up data to the cloud. SQL Server 2014 also makes it simple for SQL Server workloads to be deployed and later managed by DBAs who lack experience with Windows Azure. In addition to providing companies with more options and enabling easier administration, Microsoft is standardizing its tools so that users have a reliable and consistent experience regardless of the location from which an organization runs its data platform.

SQL Server 2014 enables hybrid solutions for data virtualization, data movement, security and availability, low-cost maintenance for high availability, and elastic scaling. The next few sections describe these new investments.

Cloud disaster recovery

As mentioned earlier, disaster recovery is easily managed by using Windows Azure. The new Add Azure Replica wizard can be used to extend an on-premises implementation of AlwaysOn Availability Groups by adding secondary replicas to Windows Azure Virtual Machines running an instance of SQL Server. Windows Azure Virtual Machines (VMs) with SQL Server can also help lower high-availability and disaster-recovery costs.

Figure 3-7 shows a hybrid IT database solution where part of the SQL Server environment runs in Windows Azure and part of the environment runs within an organization's on-premises data center.

Some of the AlwaysOn availability replicas are running in Windows Azure VMs and others are running on-premises for cross-site disaster recovery. Because all availability replicas must be in the same WSFC cluster, the WSFC cluster must span both networks and requires a VPN connection between Windows Azure and the on-premises network.

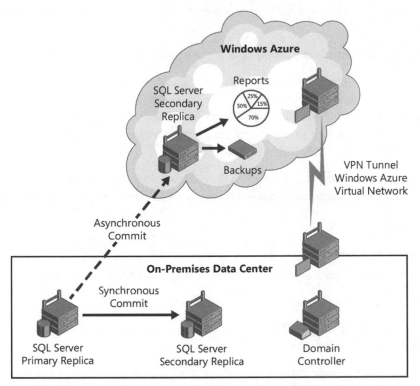

FIGURE 3-7 Using Windows Azure Virtual Machines to extend SQL Server secondary replicas in the cloud for disaster-recovery purposes.

Using the Add Azure Replica wizard

The purpose of this book is to describe the new capabilities and investments of SQL Server 2014, so we don't include step-by-step instructions for how to deploy a replica in a Windows Azure Virtual Machine. In this section, however, we provide the high-level strategy for doing so, including the prerequisites.

Prerequisites

The following prerequisites must be met to successfully deploy a replica in a Windows Azure Virtual Machine:

- The configuration requires a site-to-site VPN between Windows Azure and the on-premises network because all the replicas must be part of the same domain and multi-subnet Windows Server Failover Cluster.

- The Add Azure Replica wizard must be invoked from the SQL Server instance that is hosting the primary replica.

- A replica domain controller should be implemented in Windows Azure if you plan to use the replica as a disaster-recovery site. This is a requirement because the primary site that hosts the domain controller would not be available in the event of a primary site failure, and authentication would fail.

- The availability group must contain on-premises availability replicas.

- A Windows Azure subscription is required to generate the Windows Azure Virtual Machine and site-to-site VPN. A network share is required for the wizard to create and access backups for the initial full data synchronization. The account used to start the Database Engine must have read and write permissions to commence the operation, whereas the account used by the secondary replicas needs only read permissions.

- Clients must have Internet access to connect to the replicas in Windows Azure in the event the primary data center fails or the operations are manually failed over from on-premises to the cloud.

High-level deployment steps

Follow these steps to invoke the Add Azure Replica wizard in SQL Server Management Studio:

1. In SQL Server Management Studio, connect to the primary replica.

2. Launch the Add Azure Replica wizard by running the Availability Group wizard or the Add Replicas To Availability Group wizard.

3. On the Add Azure Replica page, click the Download button to obtain a management certificate for the Windows Azure subscription.

4. You are prompted to sign in to Windows Azure to download a management certificate. After you are authenticated, the wizard installs a management certificate on your local machine.

5. Click Connect to populate the drop-down lists with the values for the Windows Azure Virtual Network and Virtual Network Subnet options.

6. Specify settings for the new Windows Azure VM that will host the new secondary replica. The settings include:

   - **Image** Select a SQL Server image to use.

   - **VM Size** Specify the size of the Windows Azure VM.

   - **VM Name** Enter the name of the Windows Azure VM.

   - **VM Username** Enter the VM user name.

   - **VM Administrator Password** Enter the administrator password for the Windows Azure VM.

- **Confirm Password**   Confirm the password for the Windows Azure VM.

7. On the same page, enter information in the On-Premise Domain area:

    - **Domain**   The Active Directory (AD) domain to which the Windows Azure VM will be joined.

    - **Domain User Name**   The AD user name used to join the Windows Azure VM to the domain.

    - **Password**   The password used to join the Windows Azure VM to the domain.

8. Click OK to start the deployment, as illustrated in Figure 3-8.

FIGURE 3-8 Using the new Add Azure Replica wizard to create a secondary replica in Windows Azure.

9. Continue through the wizard to complete the steps on the Specify Replicas page. The steps are the same as for creating a new replica.

After you run the Availability Group wizard or the Add Replica To Availability Group wizard, a new VM is created, connected to the Active Directory domain, and added to the Windows cluster. AlwaysOn is enabled, and the new replica is added to the availability group.

Deploy a database to a Windows Azure Virtual Machine

The Deploy Database To A Windows Azure Virtual Machine wizard is another feature new in SQL Server 2014 that enhances the hybrid-cloud experience for organizations. The wizard is invoked directly from SQL Server Management Studio and used to transition databases from on-premises SQL Server instances to a Windows Azure Virtual Machine running an instance of SQL Server in the Windows Azure cloud. The wizard is fairly easy to use and requires only a few steps. Databases based on SQL Server 2008, SQL Server 2008 R2, SQL Server 2012, or SQL Server 2014 can be deployed to a Windows Azure VM by invoking the wizard from SQL Server Management Studio for SQL Server 2014. This operation has a 1-terabyte database size limitation.

Prerequisites

To deploy a database to a Windows Azure Virtual Machine, the following prerequisites must be met:

- Windows Azure subscription.

- Windows Azure publishing profile.

- A management certificate uploaded to your Windows Azure subscription.

- The management certificate must be saved in the personal certificate store on the computer on which the wizard is run.

- A temporary storage location.

High-level deployment steps

In SQL Server Management Studio, connect to an instance of SQL Server and then right-click the database you want to deploy to a Windows Azure Virtual Machine. Then follow these steps:

1. Select Tasks, and then select Deploy Database To A Windows Azure VM.

2. Review the notes and prerequisites on the Introduction page.

3. On the Source Settings page, specify the name of the instance of the SQL Server and the name of the database that will be deployed to the Windows Azure VM. Also specify a temporary location for the backup files.

4. On the Windows Azure Sign-in page, do one of the following:

   - Specify a management certificate to use when connecting to Windows Azure

   - Use a publishing profile if you already have it downloaded to your computer.

   - Click Sign In to connect to Windows Azure by using a Microsoft account to generate and download a new management certificate.

5. In the Subscription section, select or enter the Windows Azure subscription ID that matches the certificate from the local certificate store or publishing profile.

6. On the Deployment Settings page, shown in Figure 3-9, specify the Windows Azure VM that will host the database or provide a name to create a new virtual machine. In the Target Database section, select the name of the SQL Server instance you want to use and enter the name of the database. In this example, a virtual machine named SQLAzure-SQLVM is specified.

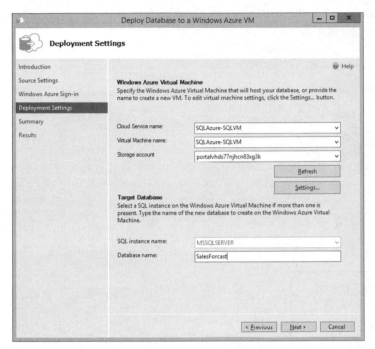

FIGURE 3-9 Specifying a Windows Azure Virtual Machine in the Deploy Database To A Windows Azure VM wizard.

7. On the Summary page, verify the choices made by the wizard, and then click Finish to commence the operations. Review the success and failure report on the Results page, and then click Finish again to close the wizard.

Storing SQL Server data files in Windows Azure

Another way for an organization to use the hybrid-cloud is to store SQL Server data and log files as blobs in Windows Azure. This approach allows SQL Server 2014 instances to be hosted within an organization's on-premises data center while SQL Server data and log files are stored in Windows Azure Blob Storage. It is worth noting that the SQL Server instances are also supported in a Windows Azure Virtual Machine and not just in on-premises data centers.

So why is this important, and what are the benefits of using Windows Azure Blob Storage? First, you can easily use the Attach and Detach functionality to move databases between SQL Server instances because the data is permanently available in the cloud. Second, Windows Azure provides unlimited storage capacity and includes built-in high availability and geo-disaster recovery. Third, for those concerned with security, the data stored in the cloud is fully encrypted through the transparent data encryption (TDE) functionality that's built in to SQL Server. Finally, a restore operation is fairly quick—it is simply an Attach operation and can be conducted on an on-premises instance of SQL Server or an instance running on a Windows Azure Virtual Machine.

Figure 3-10 illustrates a hybrid-cloud platform where an instance of SQL Server 2014 is running in an on-premises data center while the SQL Server data and log files are stored in Windows Azure Blob Storage.

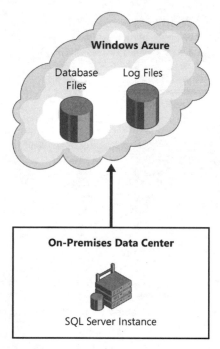

FIGURE 3-10 On-premises SQL Server instances using the Windows Azure storage service for data and log files.

Extending on-premises apps to the cloud

Another use case for building hybrid scenarios is extending on-premises SQL Server applications to the cloud. For example, an e-commerce organization that sells pizzas may want to scale its applications and infrastructure strictly for its busiest week of the year. Scaling out its on-premises applications and infrastructure for just one week might not make sense because it would significantly increase overall capital and operational expenditures, especially if the on-premises applications and infrastructure would be idle at other times throughout the remainder of the year.

In this scenario, the business would benefit from building a hybrid-cloud solution for additional scale with Windows Azure. For example, the organization could use its on-premises SQL Server and supporting infrastructure to continue to service on-site business transactions and use Windows Azure infrastructure or platform services to support online sales.

In Figure 3-11, the on-premises domain controller is used to authenticate all users (both on-premises and cloud) and is using a secure VPN tunnel to connect with the cloud instances. Also, you can use the Linked Server feature in SQL Server to make a secure connection between two instances of SQL Server and pass a transaction or a query from one SQL Server instance to another regardless of whether it is on-premises or in the cloud.

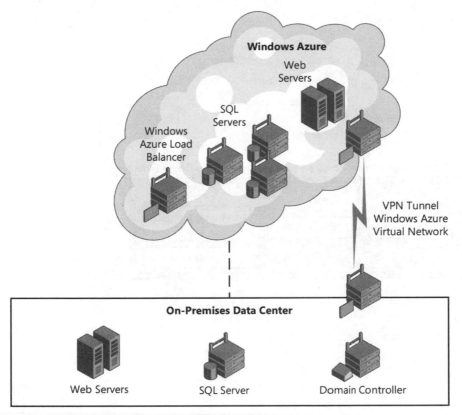

FIGURE 3-11 Extending on-premises applications to the cloud.

Backup and restore enhancements

A robust backup strategy is always required even if an organization employs high-availability, disaster-recovery, and hybrid-cloud strategies to protect its mission-critical data. SQL Server 2014 makes several investments to backup operations, including using Windows Azure for simplified backups and native encryption to protect both on-premises or cloud backups.

SQL Server backup to a URL

SQL Server 2012 SP1 CU2 enabled SQL Server backup and restore functionality to Windows Azure Blob Storage. Unfortunately, this feature was available only when issuing BACKUP and RESTORE statements with Transact-SQL, PowerShell, or SQL Server Management Objects (SMOs). In SQL Server 2014, the ability to back up to and restore from Windows Azure Blob Storage has been added to SQL Server

Management Studio via the Backup And Restore wizard and the Maintenance Plan wizard. Transact-SQL and PowerShell can still be used if you prefer them.

Figure 3-12 illustrates an on-premises SQL Server backup to Windows Azure Blob Storage by using a URL.

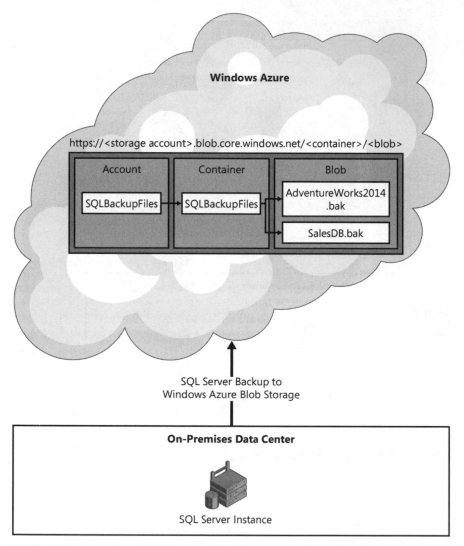

FIGURE 3-12 Leveraging the Windows Azure Blob Storage service to back up an on-premises database to Windows Azure.

Backing up SQL Server databases to the cloud offers a tremendous number of benefits to organizations, including:

- Limitless offsite storage.

- No need for backup media management.

- No hardware management overhead.

- Three copies of the data are stored in Windows Azure for redundancy, with the option for data to be replicated to a secondary location, resulting in geo-replicated offsite storage.

- Data can be quickly restored to a Windows Azure Virtual Machine in the event of a primary site disaster.

- Encryption keys can be stored on-premises, while the backup files are in the cloud.

- No need to enable transparent data encryption or use third-party solutions to encrypt backups.

To use Windows Azure Blob Storage for backups, a Windows Azure subscription is required. You need to create a storage account and a container in Windows Azure and then create a SQL Server credential that holds critical information, such as the container's policy information and an access signature that is shared. The next section illustrates how to back up to a URL by using the Backup Task in SQL Server Management Studio. Later, we show how to perform the same operation with Transact-SQL.

Backup to URL with Backup Task in SQL Server Management Studio

1. In SQL Server Management Studio, expand Databases, and then select a user database that you want to back up.

2. Right-click the database, point to Tasks, and then click Back Up.

3. On the General page, specify the backup options you would usually select, such as backup type and backup component. To use Windows Azure Blob Storage, select URL in the Backup To list in the Destination section.

4. For the additional URL options on the page, enter the following information, as illustrated in Figure 3-13:

   - **File Name**   Enter the name of the backup file, such as SaleForcast_Backup.bak

   - **SQL Credential**   Enter or select an existing SQL Server credential, or create a new one by clicking Create.

   - **Azure Storage Container**   Specify the name of the Windows Azure storage container where you will store the backup files, such as SalesForcastDB

   - **URL Prefix**   The URL prefix is built automatically using the information specified in the fields described earlier. If you edit this value, be sure it matches the other information you provided. For example, if you modify the storage URL, be sure that SQL Credential is set to authenticate to the same storage account.

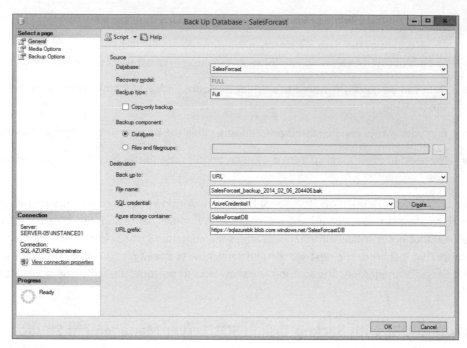

FIGURE 3-13 Using the Back Up Database wizard to backup an on-premises database to Windows Azure using a URL prefix.

5. On the Media Options and Backup Options pages, enter additional backup information, such as reliability options, compression, and encryption.

Backing up to a URL by using Transact-SQL

The following Transact-SQL example illustrates how to back up a SQL Server database to a URL.

```
BACKUP DATABASE [SalesForcast]
TO  URL =
N'https://sqlazurebk.blob.core.windows.net/SalesForcastDB/SalesForcast_
backup_2014_02_06_204406.bak' WITH  CREDENTIAL = N'AzureCredential1' , NOFORMAT, NOINIT,
NAME = N'SalesForcast-Full Database Backup', NOSKIP, NOREWIND, NOUNLOAD,  STATS = 10
GO
```

Encryption for backups

For many years, organizations and customers have requested that native encryption for backups be included with SQL Server. In the past, encryption for backups could be achieved through third-party solutions or with transparent data encryption (TDE). Third-party solutions added additional costs to the overall solution, and TDE would encrypt not only the backup but the whole database, which was not always a requirement of an organization or practical, given the additional administrative and performance overhead.

In SQL Server 2014, organizations can encrypt data while creating a backup. This is achieved by specifying the encryption algorithm and the encryptor when you create the backup. Encrypted backups are supported whether you create the backup on-premises or with Windows Azure. In addition, encryption can be applied when you use the Back Up Database wizard, the Maintenance Plan wizard, or with Transact-SQL.

Creating a database master key

The first step in successfully encrypting a backup file is to create a database master key. The following Transact-SQL example creates a database master key and stores the complex password in the database.

```
-- Creates a database master key.
-- The key is encrypted using the password "<master key password>"
USE master;
GO
CREATE MASTER KEY ENCRYPTION BY PASSWORD = '2.48h]zD>qJ~NfL_L6dh';
GO
```

Creating a backup certificate

The next step is to create the backup certificate in the master database. The following Transact-SQL example creates a certificate named MyDBBackupEncryptCert.

```
Use Master
GO
CREATE CERTIFICATE MyDBBackupEncryptCert
    WITH SUBJECT = 'MyDB Backup Encryption Certificate';
GO
```

Encrypting the backup by using the Backup Database wizard in SQL Server Management Studio

Follow these steps to encrypt a database by using the Backup Database wizard:

1. In SQL Server Management Studio, expand Databases, and then select the user database you want to back up. In this example, the database named SalesForcast is used.

2. Right-click the database, point to Tasks, and then click Back Up.

3. On the General page, specify the backup options you would usually select, such as backup type, backup component, and destination. For this example, a full database backup will be conducted and the destination will be disk.

4. On the Backup Options page, set Encrypt Backup to true. Please note that the encryption option is available only when Back Up To A New Media set is selected in Media Options.

5. Select an encryption algorithm to use for the encryption step, and provide a certificate or an asymmetric key from a list of existing certificates or asymmetric keys. For this example, AES 128 and the certificate MyDBBackupEncryptCert, which was created in the previous example, are selected, as shown in Figure 3-14.

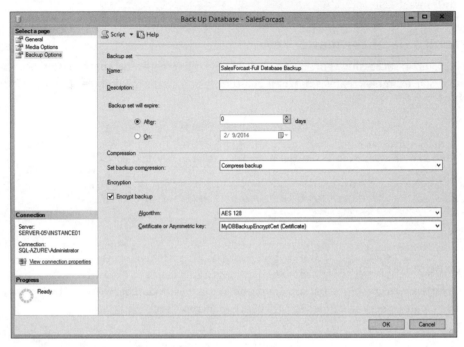

FIGURE 3-14 Specifying the encryption type and certificate or asymmetric key to encrypt a database backup.

Encrypting the backup by using Transact-SQL

The following Transact-SQL statement would encrypt the backup based on the inputs specified in the preceding example:

```
BACKUP DATABASE [SalesForcast]
TO  DISK = N'C:\Temp\db_backup_cxvirmpz.wtq.bak'
WITH FORMAT, INIT,
MEDIANAME = N'SalesForcastMediaSet',
NAME = N'SalesForcast-Full Database Backup',
SKIP, NOREWIND, NOUNLOAD,
COMPRESSION,
ENCRYPTION(ALGORITHM = AES_128,
SERVER CERTIFICATE = [MyDBBackupEncryptCert]),  STATS = 10
GO
```

SQL Server Managed Backup to Windows Azure

SQL Server 2014 introduces SQL Server Managed Backup to Windows Azure to further save on storage and administration while achieving additional offsite data protection with the Windows Azure Blob Storage service. SQL Server Managed Backup to Windows Azure is a SQL Server feature that automates database backup and maintains the backups based on the retention period. When using this new functionality, there isn't a need to manage backup policies, and the backup strategy measures database usage patterns to set the frequency of backups to Windows Azure. The main differentiators and benefits for SQL Server Managed Backup to Windows Azure compared with traditional backups to the cloud include the following:

- Currently automating backups for multiple databases requires developing a backup strategy, writing custom code, and scheduling backups.

- SQL Server Managed Backup to Windows Azure can be configured at the database or instance level. If configured at the instance level, the settings are applicable to any database created thereafter.

- Additional granular control can be achieved for each database backup because you can override default instance-level settings when creating policies at the database level. For example, setting the retention period at the database level allows you to override the default settings at the instance level

- You specify the retention period, and SQL Server Managed Backup to Windows Azure determines the type and frequency of backups for a database and stores the backups on the Windows Azure Blob Storage service. The supported values are in the range of 1-30 days.

- When a backup is configured to use encryption, you have additional security for the backed-up data.

Enabling SQL Server Managed Backup to Windows Azure at the instance level

The system stored procedure smart_backup.set_instance_backup is used to enable SQL Server Managed Backup to Windows Azure and configure the default settings at the instance level. The value 1 must be specified for the @enable_backup parameter to enable backups and set the default configurations. As indicated earlier, once the settings have been configured at the instance level, the settings will be applied to all new databases created on this same instance. The following items need to be specified as well: retention period (from 1 to 30 days), the SQL credential used to authenticate to the Windows Azure storage account, and whether to use encryption.

The following Transact-SQL syntax can be used to enable SQL Server Managed Backup to Windows Azure at the instance level. A retention period of 30 days and AES 128 encryption have been specified.

```
Use msdb;
Go
EXEC smart_admin.sp_set_instance_backup
```

```
                    @storage_url = 'https://mystorageaccount.blob.core.windows.net'
                    ,@retention_days=30
                    ,@credential_name='MyCredential'
                    ,@encryption_algorithm ='AES_128'
                    ,@encryptor_type= 'Certificate'
                    ,@encryptor_name='MyBackupCert'
                    ,@enable_backup=1;
GO
```

Enabling SQL Server Managed Backup to Windows Azure for a database

The system stored procedure smart_admin.sp_set_db_backup is used to enable SQL Server Managed Backup to Windows Azure for a specific database. The following items need to be specified along with enabling the backup: the name of the database, the retention period from 1 to 30 days, the SQL credential used to authenticate to the Windows Azure storage account, and whether to encrypt the backups.

The following Transact-SQL syntax can be used to enable SQL Server Managed Backup to Windows Azure at the database level. A retention period of 30 days and AES 256 encryption have been specified.

```
Use msdb;
GO
EXEC smart_admin.sp_set_db_backup
                @database_name='TestDB'
                ,@enable_backup=1,
                ,@storage_url = 'https://mystorageaccount.blob.core.windows.net'
                ,@retention_days =30
                ,@credential_name ='MyCredential'
                ,@encryption_algorithm ='AES_256'
                ,@encryptor_type= 'Certificate'
                ,@encryptor_name='MyBackupCert'

GO
```

Business intelligence development

Exploring self-service BI in Microsoft Excel 2013

Self-service business intelligence (BI) is not new to Microsoft Excel. Since Excel 2000, users have been able to connect to an Analysis Services cube to explore data by using PivotTables and PivotCharts. In Excel 2010, PowerPivot was introduced as an add-in based on SQL Server technology. PowerPivot permitted users to import data from a variety of sources and develop a model defining relationships and calculations that users could then explore by using PivotTables and PivotCharts. In Excel 2013, PowerPivot is still available with some new capabilities, but several other features in Excel make exploring and interacting with data even easier: Excel Data Model, Power Query, Power View, and Power Map.

Excel Data Model and Power Pivot

In Excel 2013, PowerPivot is built into Excel, so you aren't required to download and install the add-in, but this applies only to specific versions: Office Professional Plus 2013, Office 365 Professional Plus, and the standalone edition of Excel 2013. When Power BI was announced as a new service for Office 365, PowerPivot was rebranded as Power Pivot, although for now this new name appears only in online documentation because the rebranding occurred after Excel 2013 was released. All references in the product's user interface continue to display PowerPivot. Nonetheless, from this point forward in this book we use the new name, Power Pivot.

As part of the integration of Power Pivot into Excel, a type of object called a Data Model was also introduced. You can think of this object as a light version of Power Pivot. It provides storage for data that you import and contains metadata about that data, such as relationships between tables, but it does not contain enhancements to the data, such as calculated columns or column properties that require Power Pivot features. On the other hand, it does use the same built-in xVelocity engine (formerly known as Vertipaq) that was added to Excel 2010 to support Power Pivot. This means that your data is stored in a highly compressed, columnar, in-memory format that is efficient to query.

Working with the Data Model

A Data Model is created when you select the Add This Data To The Data Model check box in the Import Data dialog box. This check box is automatically selected, without the option to clear it (as shown in Figure 4-1), when you import multiple tables with one connection. However, if you import only a single table, the check box is not selected, and you must explicitly select it to add the table data to the Data Model.

FIGURE 4-1 The Import Data dialog box with the Add This Data To The Data Model check box selected.

You can continue to import data from other sources and add that data to the Data Model. If you import data without adding it to the Data Model, you can add it later. To do this, first highlight the cells that you want to add or place your cursor in one of the cells of a table or named range that contains your data. Next, click Add To Data Model on the Power Pivot tab on the ribbon or click PivotTable on the Insert tab and then select the Add This Data To The Data Model check box in the Create PivotTable dialog box.

Note There is only one Data Model per Excel workbook.

When you have multiple tables in the Data Model, you can import relationships when you import the tables from a relational source as a group. Otherwise, you can manually define the relationships between tables when you want to include data from them in a single report. Click Relationships on the Data tab to open the Manage Relationships dialog box, and then click New. Select the table containing the foreign column (that is, the column with values repeating across multiple rows) and the foreign column in the top row, and then select the related table and primary column (that is, the column with distinct values only), as shown in Figure 4-2.

The tables and fields that you add to the Data Model are visible in the Field List when you add a PivotTable, a PivotChart, or a Power View report to the workbook. The result is the same if you import data by using Power Pivot features and then define relationships. The key difference between the Data Model and Power Pivot is the inability to rename tables and columns or use the advanced modeling features of Power Pivot when your data is in the Data Model only. However, the Data Model is an easy way to start interactively exploring data without much effort. You can always open the Power Pivot interface to apply Power Pivot features to the model if additional refinement proves necessary.

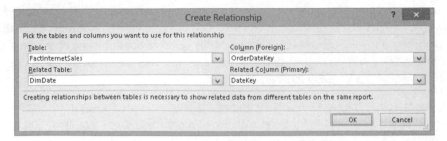

FIGURE 4-2 Create Relationship dialog box displaying selection of tables and columns for a new relationship.

After building your first PivotTable or other type of report based on the Data Model, you can create another report based on the same Data Model. On the Insert tab, click PivotTable. Then, in the Create PivotTable dialog box, select Use An External Data Source, click Choose Connection, click the Tables tab, and select Tables In Workbook Data Model, as shown in Figure 4-3.

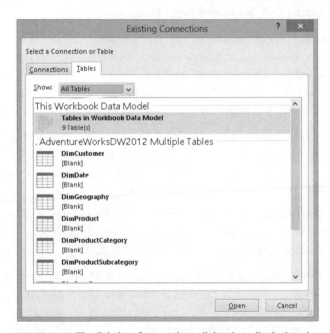

FIGURE 4-3 The Existing Connections dialog box displaying the selection of Tables In Workbook Data Model.

Managing data as a Power Pivot model

When you need to refine the Data Model in some way, you need to use Power Pivot. You might do this when you need to import a subset of data. Power Pivot allows you to select specific columns for import or to apply a filter to import a selected set of rows. After you import data, you can rename tables and columns, create relationships, and add formatting to improve the display of data in reports.

You can also enhance the data with calculations to perform arithmetic or statistical operations or even to cleanse the data, such as replacing empty values with a default string or number.

The SQL Server 2012 release of Power Pivot for Excel is available as a downloadable add-in for Excel 2010, but it is built directly into Excel 2013. In either version of Excel, Power Pivot must be enabled. To do this, click Options on the File tab in Excel, select Add-Ins in the navigation pane of the Excel Options dialog box, select COM Add-ins in the Manage drop-down list, click the Go button, and select the Microsoft Office PowerPivot for Excel 2013 (or 2010) check box.

The latest release of Power Pivot in Excel 2013 works much like it did when it was introduced as part of SQL Server 2008 R2, as an add-in for Excel 2010. However, the workbook size limitation has been removed from the 64-bit version of Excel, which means your workbook can be as large as the amount of disk and memory on your computer permits. As you might expect, there are several new features, some changed features, and a few features that have been removed, as described in the following list:

- **Calculated fields**   Instead of right-clicking a table in the Field List to add a calculated field (previously called a measure), you click Calculated Fields on the Power Pivot tab (although you can still create a calculated field in the Calculation Area in the Power Pivot window).

- **Perspectives**   The list of available perspectives is no longer available at the top of the Field List. Now you can use perspectives to view a subset of the model only when you have the Power Pivot window open. If you publish your workbook to Power Pivot for SharePoint, you can create a connection string that uses the perspective explicitly. In addition to the Data Source and Initial Catalog keywords in the connection string, add *Cube=<perspective name>*.

- **KPIs**   In the previous version, you could select a calculated field in the Field List to enable the Create KPI option on the Power Pivot tab. Now you can use the KPIs option to create a new KPI or manage existing KPIs without making a selection in the Field List. You still have the ability to create a KPI in the Calculation Area in the Power Pivot window.

- **Descriptions**   You no longer view descriptions for tables, columns, and calculated fields in the Field List when working with a PivotTable or PivotChart. A description is now displayed only as a ScreenTip in the Field List of a Power View report.

- **Slicers**   The Slicers Vertical and Slicers Horizontal areas are no longer displayed at the bottom of the Field List. Instead, you right-click the field in the Field List and then select Add As Slicer from the submenu. To change the orientation of the slicer, click the slicer to select it, and then click Align Vertically or Align Horizontally on the Power Pivot tab.

- **Search**   The Search box has been removed from the Field List. Instead, use the Find option on the Home tab in the Power Pivot window to search for a table, column, or calculated field by name.

- **Relationships**   Power Pivot is no longer capable of automatically detecting relationships between tables. You must import relationships when importing a group of tables at one time or manually define the relationships in the model.

- **Data categorization** The Advanced tab on the ribbon in the Power Pivot window includes a Data Category list that you use to assign one of the following categories to a column: Address, City, Company, Continent, Country/Region, Country, Date, Image, Image URL, Latitude, Longitude, Organization, Place, Postal Code, Product, State Or Province, or Web URL. Power View uses this categorization to apply the proper visualization to your data where possible. In addition, Windows Azure Marketplace uses this information to suggest data sources that might be useful to integrate into your Power Pivot model.

Upgrading from PowerPivot for Excel 2010

To upgrade an existing workbook that was created in Excel 2010, first open the workbook in Excel 2013. On the Power Pivot tab, click Manage. Excel displays a message explaining that you must upgrade the data model before using Power Pivot for Excel 2013. Click OK to display another message that warns that the upgraded workbook cannot be used with previous versions of Power Pivot. Click OK to start the upgrade. When the upgrade is complete, another message prompts you to take the workbook out of Excel compatibility mode. Click Yes to save, close, and reopen the workbook and thereby exit Excel compatibility mode.

Power Query

Power Pivot is a great tool for gathering together data from disparate sources and combining it into a single model for analysis, but it presumes you know that the data exists, where to find it, and how to use DAX to create calculated columns for simple restructuring or cleansing of your data. For discovering data and to use more advanced techniques for transforming data, you can use Power Query. Power Query is a separate downloadable add-in for the following Excel versions: Office Professional Plus 2013, Office 365 Professional Plus, and the standalone edition of Excel 2013.

Note You can download Power Query for Excel (32-bit or 64-bit) from *http://www. microsoft.com/en-us/download/details.aspx?id=39379* for the January 2014 release, although a newer version might be available. Search for Power Query in the Microsoft Download Center (*http://www.microsoft.com/en-us/download*) to locate the latest version by release date. You can also install this add-in for Excel 2010 if you are using Microsoft Office Professional Plus 2010 with Software Assurance through Volume Licensing.

At a minimum, you use Power Query to find data that you need and then view it in a table after filtering it and shaping it to meet your requirements. You can also load the data retrieved by Power Query into the Data Model so that you can build PivotTables, PivotCharts, or Power View reports. Of course, after the data is in the Data Model, you can further enhance it by using Power Pivot. If you have an Office 365 subscription with Power BI enabled, you can share the queries that you develop, find and use existing shared queries, and monitor the use of shared queries.

Searching for data

One of the distinguishing features of Power Query is its ability to help you find not only internal data sources (if your organization uses Power BI) but also data from public data sources. Internal data sources are curated queries that designated users publish for others to use. To use this feature, you must click Sign In on the Power Query tab on the ribbon and enter your Office 365 logon credentials. Currently, public data sources include only sources based in the United States. The current collection that you can search (subject to change) includes the following data sources:

- Dun & Bradstreet financial data (sample data only)

- HealthData.gov

- MCH Strategic Data (sample data only)

- Open Government data (Data.gov)

- Wikipedia

- Windows Azure Marketplace

- The World Bank

You start a search by clicking Online Search on the Power Query tab. You then type one or more keywords in the search box. If you used the Sign In button to log on to Office 365, a drop-down list appears to the right of the search box that allows you to restrict your search by choosing one of the following options:

- **All**   This is the default selection, with no restriction on which data sources to search.

- **My Shared**   This selection forces Power Query to search only the shared queries that you have published to Power BI. Shared queries are explained in more detail in the "Shared queries" section in Chapter 5, "Introducing Power BI for Office 365."

- **Public**   When you select this option, Power Query returns only a set of public data sources.

- **Organization**   With this selection, Power Query includes all shared queries that you have permission to see, whether created by you or someone else.

A list of results is displayed as a series of pages in the Online Search pane, as shown in Figure 4-4. When you point to one of the results, a preview flyout screen displays a sample of the selected data source, in addition to a list of the columns the data source contains, the last modified date, the name of the source, and a link to the source. Your search keywords are highlighted in yellow.

At the bottom of the preview flyout screen, you can click Add To Worksheet to import the data unchanged into a new worksheet. If you need to modify the data first, click Edit instead. Then you can perform one or more of the steps described in the "Shaping data" section later in this chapter.

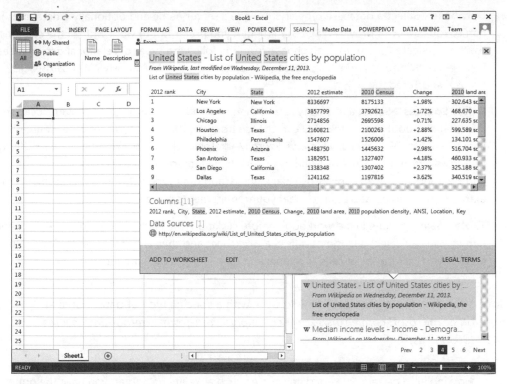

FIGURE 4-4 Power Query online search results.

Importing data

If you already know where to find the data you want, you can import it directly without performing a search. To do this, click the applicable option for your data source type in the Get External Data group on the Power Query tab (shown in Figure 4-5), and then select the data source.

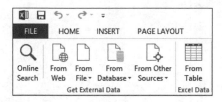

FIGURE 4-5 Get External Data options on the Power Query tab.

You can import from the following types of data sources:

- **Web**   Provide the URL for a webpage containing data in a table format that Power Query can scrape or for a supported file type stored on a web server.

- **File**   Select a file type and then browse to the file location to select it. You can choose from the following types of files: Excel, CSV, XML, and text. You can even import metadata about files stored in a folder, such as file name, file name extension, date modified, and path.

- **Database** Select a database type and provide a server name and optionally a database name. You can even provide a SQL statement if you prefer not to work with all the columns or rows of a selected table. You can choose from the following types of relational data sources: SQL Server, Windows Azure SQL Database, Access, Oracle, IBM DB2, MySQL, PostgreSQL, Sybase, and Teradata.

- **Other Sources** Select a source type and then respond to the prompt to provide location information about the source. You can choose from the following types of other sources: SharePoint list, OData feed, Windows Azure Marketplace, Hadoop, Windows Azure HDInsight, Windows Azure Blob Storage, Windows Azure Table Storage, Active Directory, Exchange, and Facebook. You can also choose Blank Query and then type a Power Query formula that extracts and manipulates data to meet your requirements more specifically.

- **Table** Select a table in the workbook before clicking From Table on the ribbon. As an alternative, you can select a range of cells in a worksheet and then click From Table. Power Query first converts the range of cells to a table and then imports the data into a query.

> **Note** You can learn more about how to work with a specific type of data source at *http://office.microsoft.com/en-us/excel-help/import-data-from-external-data-sources-HA104003952.aspx.*

When working with certain types of data sources, such as relational tables, you have the option to import multiple items from the same source, as shown in Figure 4-6, by selecting the Select Multiple Items check box at the top of the Navigator pane. You can then select the check box for each item to import. When you point to a single item, a preview flyout screen displays a sampling of the data. A separate query is added to the workbook for each item you choose to load.

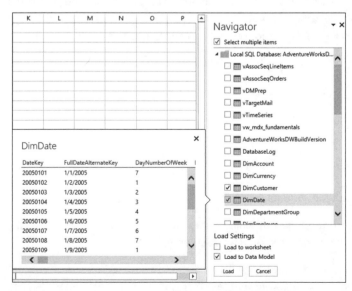

FIGURE 4-6 Select multiple items from a source in the Navigator pane and preview data in a selected item.

Note If you import multiple related tables from a relational source at the same time, Power Query detects the existing relationships and automatically adds them to the Data Model. However, if you import more related tables later, any existing relationships between the previously imported tables and the currently selected tables are ignored and not imported into the Data Model.

Loading the worksheet or Data Model

When you finish working with a query, you have the options to load the data into a worksheet only, into the Excel Data Model only, or to both locations. If you want to use the data with Power View or Power Map, you must load the data into the Data Model. This option is not enabled until the download of data from the data source is complete. You use the check boxes at the bottom of the Query Settings pane to make your selection, as shown in Figure 4-7.

◢ **LOAD SETTINGS**
☑ Load to worksheet
☑ Load to Data Model

FIGURE 4-7 Load settings in the Query Settings pane.

Shaping data

After using the online search option or importing data, you can manipulate the data in a variety of ways, reshaping the data by applying a series of transformations, filtering it, and splitting columns, to name just a few operations. If you import multiple data sets that share common data columns, you can combine these data sets into a single table to make analyzing the data easier.

To shape data for a particular query, you must open the Query Editor. You can do this by clicking Workbook in the Manage Queries group on the Power Query tab and then double-clicking the query in the Workbook Queries pane. Another way to open the Query Editor is to open the worksheet containing the table of data associated with the query, click the Query tab below the Table Tools tab, and then click Edit Query on the ribbon. You can then use options on the Query Editor ribbon, shown in Figure 4-8, to reduce the number of rows or columns in the query results, sort data, apply a transformation such as splitting a column, create a new column, or combine data from multiple queries by merging or appending data. You can also launch these operations by right-clicking a row or column to display a submenu of commands.

FIGURE 4-8 The Query Editor ribbon.

The process of shaping data can involve one or more steps. As a simple example, let's look at the data from an online search, shown in Figure 4-9. In this example, the 2010 Land Area column contains data for both square miles and square kilometers, which can better be used in reports if the data is split into separate columns and restricted to the numeric portion of the data. Another column (not visible) contains latitude and longitude information that should likewise be separated.

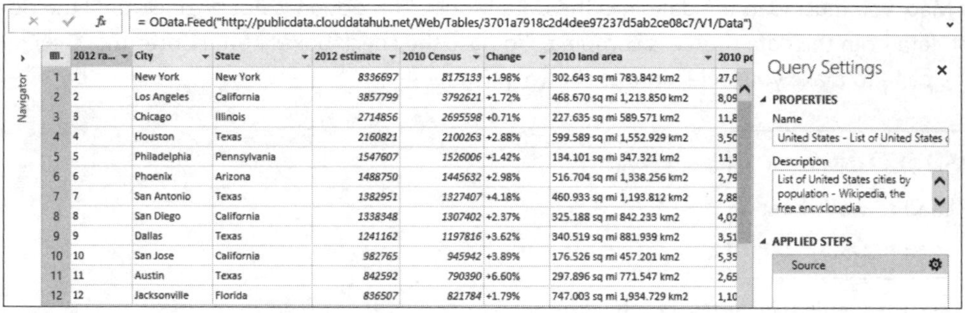

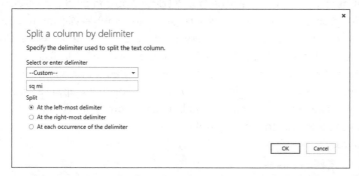

FIGURE 4-9 Data in the Query Editor before transformation.

To edit the query, select the column in the grid and then use the ribbon or the submenu that is displayed when you right-click the column to apply a new step. For example, to separate the data in the 2010 Land Area column, you can use the Split Column By Delimiter transformation. When you specify this type of transformation, a dialog box prompts you for more instructions. In this case, you must choose Custom in the Select Or Enter Delimiter list, type **sq mi** in the next box, and then specify the position of the delimiter to use for splitting, as shown in Figure 4-10.

FIGURE 4-10 The Split A Column By Delimiter dialog box displaying a custom delimiter definition.

When you close the dialog box, Power Query creates two columns with the same name and a numeric value appended to uniquely identify each column, as shown in Figure 4-11. At this point, you can rename the columns to more clearly distinguish between the two and continue to apply transformations to produce query results that are more useful in reports.

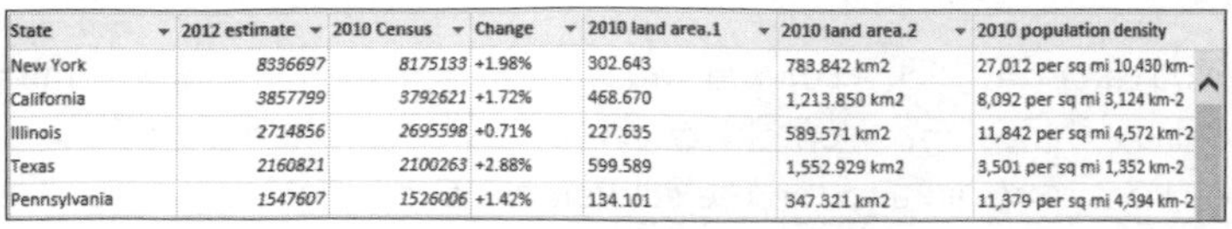

State	2012 estimate	2010 Census	Change	2010 land area.1	2010 land area.2	2010 population density
New York	8336697	8175133	+1.98%	302.643	783.842 km2	27,012 per sq mi 10,430 km-
California	3857799	3792621	+1.72%	468.670	1,213.850 km2	8,092 per sq mi 3,124 km-2
Illinois	2714856	2695598	+0.71%	227.635	589.571 km2	11,842 per sq mi 4,572 km-2
Texas	2160821	2100263	+2.88%	599.589	1,552.929 km2	3,501 per sq mi 1,352 km-2
Pennsylvania	1547607	1526006	+1.42%	134.101	347.321 km2	11,379 per sq mi 4,394 km-2

FIGURE 4-11 Query results after applying the Split Column By Delimiter transformation

Power Query includes the following types of transformations for cleansing and restructuring your data:

- **Filter**   Click the arrow icon in a column to display a list of distinct values in the column, and then select the values to keep in the query results. You also have access to text, number, or date filters, just as you do when you use the Excel filter feature on a regular worksheet column. Another way to filter is to right-click a cell containing a value that you want to keep in or exclude from the results, point to Text Filters (or Number Filters or Date Filters), and then select a comparison operator such as Equals or Does Not Equal, among others. The comparison operator is applied to the selected cell value, and the rows are filtered according to the criteria you set.

- **Sort**   Select a column, and then click Sort Ascending or Sort Descending on the Query Editor ribbon. If you continue by applying a sort direction to additional columns, the initial sort remains intact, and the additional columns are sorted in the order selected. Click the arrow icon in the column and select Clear Sort to remove the sort transformation from the query steps.

- **Group rows**   Click Group By on the Query Editor ribbon, and then select one or more fields to use for grouping rows. You must provide a name for a new column that's created to hold the aggregated value for the grouped rows, select the aggregate function to use (such as Sum or Count Rows), and specify the column to be aggregated.

- **Expand column**   Certain operations return a column of complex values, which is analogous to associating a table of columns and rows with each row in the data grid. You can click the expand icon in the column header and then select the columns to add to the data grid. The expand icon looks like this:

- **Aggregate**   When you have a column of complex values, click the expand icon in the column header, select the Aggregate option button in the column drop-down list, point to one of the aggregate functions (such as Sum of SalesAmount), and then select one or more of the available aggregation functions: Sum, Average, Minimum, Maximum, Count (All), and Count (Not Blank).

- **Insert index or custom column**   You can add an index column by clicking Insert Index Column on the Query Editor ribbon. Each row is numbered consecutively, beginning with zero for the first row. Another option is to create a column to contain values calculated from a query formula that you define. Click Insert Custom Column to open a query formula box for the new column and then provide a query formula to calculate a result for each row in the column.

- **Remove column(s)**   You can right-click a column you want to delete and then select Remove on the submenu to eliminate the column from the query results. As an alternative, you can right-click a column you want to retain and then select Remove Other Columns to reduce the query results to the single column you selected.

- **Remove error rows**   When you want to eliminate rows containing errors from the query results, right-click a column containing error rows and select Remove Errors on the submenu.

- **Promote row to column headers**   If the first row of the data grid contains column headers, click the table icon in the upper-left corner of the grid, and then select Use First Row As Headers in the submenu.

- **Split column**   Separate a single column into two or more columns by using delimiters or a fixed number of characters.

- **Merge column**   The merge operation requires all columns to have the text data type, so you might need to change the data type of some columns first. Select the column, and then select a data type in the Data Type list on the Query Editor ribbon. While pressing the Ctrl key, select two or more columns to merge, and then select a separator to insert between column values, such as a comma or a space. A new column replaces the selected columns in the query results. If you prefer to create a new column with the merged column values, click Insert Custom Column on the Query Editor ribbon and use a formula to concatenate columns, like this: =[City] & " " & [State]

As you perform each operation on the data, notice that new steps appear in the Query Settings pane. Figure 4-12 shows the set of steps required to reshape the 2010 Land Area and Location columns. You can click any of the steps to see the shape of the data after the selected step was applied. If you try a transformation that fails to produce the result you want, you can delete the step by clicking the X icon that is displayed to the left of the step when you point to the step's name. If you need to change a step setting, such as a delimiter value for the Split Column By Delimiter transformation, click the gear icon to the right of the step's name.

FIGURE 4-12 The Query Settings pane displaying a series of transformation steps applied to a query.

As you select a step in the Query Settings pane, the formula bar above the data grid displays the query formula, as shown in Figure 4-13. After you learn the Power Query Formula Language, you can build more complex expressions and customize a transformation to better meet your needs.

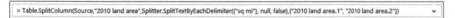

= Table.SplitColumn(Source,"2010 land area",Splitter.SplitTextByEachDelimiter({"sq mi"}, null, false),{"2010 land area.1", "2010 land area.2"})

FIGURE 4-13 The formula bar displaying an example of a query formula for a Split Column By Delimiter transformation.

> **Note** More information about the Power Query Formula Language is available at *http://office.microsoft.com/en-us/excel-help/learn-about-power-query-formulas-HA104003958.aspx.*

When you finish editing a query, confirm that you have selected the correct Load Settings and then click Apply & Close on the Query Editor ribbon. The data loads as a table in a worksheet, as a table in the Data Model, or both, depending on your Load Settings selections.

Combining data

If your workbook contains two or more queries that have a column in common—such as when one query returns Sales Header data and another query returns Sales Detail with a common sales order number column in each query—you can use an inline merge to merge data as a step in a single query. You do this by clicking the table icon in the upper-left corner of the grid and then selecting Merge. Your other option is to use an intermediate merge to create a separate query for each merge, which you launch by opening the query to use as the primary table and then clicking Merge on the Query Editor ribbon. In the latter case, your workbook contains multiple queries.

Whichever option you use, you select the second table for the merge operation in the Merge dialog box and then select the matching column(s) for the primary and secondary tables, as shown in Figure 4-14. Power Query compares the data in both tables to determine how many rows match, which helps you judge the quality of the merge operation. By default, the Only Include Matching Rows check box is not selected, which means the query results might contain rows for which the columns from the secondary table are null when no match exists between the tables, similar to a left outer join in a relational query. However, if you select this check box, the query results contain only rows that match, which could be fewer than the number of rows in the primary table, similar to an inner join in a relational query.

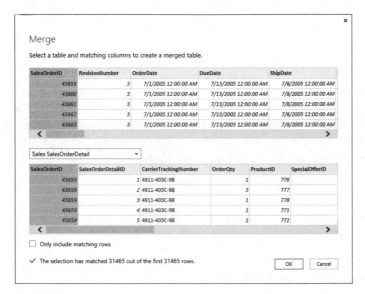

FIGURE 4-14 The Merge dialog box displaying a selection of common columns for primary and secondary tables.

When you click OK in the Merge dialog box as a step in an intermediate merge operation, a new Query Editor window opens to display the query results for the new query. You must then expand the table link column—the last column in the data grid—to add the new columns into the grid alongside the columns from the primary table.

Instead of expanding an existing query by adding columns from a second query, you can expand the existing query by adding rows from a second query, which you achieve by performing an append operation. As for a merge operation, you can choose an inline append or an intermediate append. Launch an inline append operation by clicking the table icon in the upper-left corner of the data grid and then selecting Append. To launch an intermediate append operation, click Append on the Power Query ribbon. Either way, launching the append operation opens the Append dialog box, in which you must specify the secondary table to append to the primary table. When you click OK, the query results are displayed in the data grid.

Power View

Power View in SharePoint was introduced in SQL Server 2012 as a feature in the SharePoint integrated mode of Reporting Services. Much of the functionality in that version of Power View (described in our previous book, *Introducing Microsoft SQL Server 2012*, published by Microsoft Press in 2012) is available now in Excel 2013 as a built-in add-in that you must enable as described earlier in this chapter for the Power Pivot add-in. Power View in Excel also includes the features added to Power View in SQL Server 2012 Service Pack 1, such as maps, hierarchies, and themes.

> **Note** The two features available in Power View in SharePoint that are not available in Power View in Excel are the ability to develop reports using an Analysis Services multidimensional model as a source and the ability to export the report to Microsoft PowerPoint format. Also, unlike the Power Pivot and Power Query add-ins, which you can install in Excel 2010, the Power View add-in works only with Excel 2013. Like Power View in SharePoint, Power View in Excel requires you to install Silverlight.

Creating a Power View report

As we mentioned at the beginning of this chapter, Excel has one Data Model per workbook. You can insert a Power View report into a workbook based on this model or on an external data source. By using the external data source option, you can add different Power View reports that rely on separate data sources to the same workbook.

To create a Power View report, click Power View on the Insert tab on the ribbon. A special sheet is displayed in the workbook, with a report design surface and a filters pane. Select fields in the Power View Fields list to add a table to the report design surface. You can click the Design tab on the ribbon to switch to one of the following data visualizations, all of which are also in the Power View in Share-Point version:

- Matrix

- Card

- Bar (stacked, 100% stacked, clustered)

- Column (stacked, 100% stacked, clustered)

- Line

- Scatter

- Pie

- Map

Note Like Power Pivot, Power View is not a new self-service BI feature, although it is new to Excel. Because we have elected to dedicate the majority of this chapter to new features, we do not repeat the information we provided on this topic in *Introducing Microsoft SQL Server 2012*. You can learn more about the features added as part of SQL Server 2012 SP1 at *http://office.microsoft.com/en-us/excel-help/whats-new-in-power-view-in-excel-2013-and-in-sharepoint-server-HA102901475.aspx#_Toc358038111*.

Working with visualizations

To start a new visualization on the same report, click an empty area of the report and begin selecting fields to add to the new table, which you can switch to a new visualization later. You can also create a visualization by copying an existing visualization and pasting it into the same sheet. After you paste the copy, you can change the fields selected in the bottom section of the Power View Fields list to arrange the visualization to suit your needs, as shown in Figure 4-15. You can also copy and paste visualizations from one sheet to another, but only if you are working with the same data connection on both sheets.

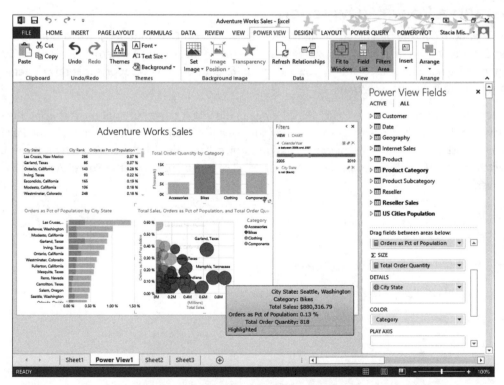

FIGURE 4-15 A Power View report in Excel with multiple visualizations on a single sheet.

Sharing a Power View report

After designing a Power View report in Excel, you can publish it to Excel Services as part of an on-premises SharePoint infrastructure or to Office 365 as part of a cloud infrastructure. If publishing your workbook to an on-premises SharePoint installation, you can add it to a standard SharePoint document library or to the Power Pivot Gallery. If you choose the Power Pivot Gallery, the thumbnail image for the Power View report is not displayed in the gallery views, although the Power View report displays normally when you open the workbook from that location. We describe the user experience for viewing a Power View report in the cloud in the "Power BI sites" and "Power BI for Mobile" sections in Chapter 5.

Power Map

As a three-dimensional (3-D) spatial-visualization tool, Power Map adds location context to your business metrics and even allows you to see how these metrics change by location over time. Like Power Query, Power Map is a separate downloadable add-in that you must enable in Excel after installing it. (Enabling an add-in is described in the "Managing data as a Power Pivot model" section earlier in this chapter.) To use Power Map, you must install one of the following versions of Microsoft Office on your computer:

- Office Professional Plus 2013

- Office 365 ProPlus

- Office 365 Midsize Business

- Office 365 E3, E4, A3, A4, G3, or G4

> **Note** You can download Power Map Preview for Excel (32-bit or 64-bit) from *http://www.microsoft.com/en-us/download/details.aspx?id=38395* for the September 2013 release, although a newer version might be available. Search for Power Map in the Microsoft Download Center (*http://www.microsoft.com/en-us/download*) to locate the latest version by release date. Unlike for Power Query, you cannot also install this add-in for Excel 2010.
>
> Although a 32-bit version of Power Map is available, you should use a 64-bit computer if you will be analyzing large volumes of data. With a 32-bit computer, you need a minimum of 1 GB of RAM, but a 64-bit computer should have at least 2 GB of RAM.

For greatest precision, you can include latitude and longitude data in your data set, but Power Map can identify and geocode locations in a table, a Data Model, or a Power Pivot model based on the following types of geographic data:

- Street Address

- City

- County

- State/Province

- Zip Code/Postal Code

- Country/Region

 Important Your computer must have Internet connectivity to use Power Map because the geocoding in Power Map relies on the Bing Maps service.

Creating a Power Map

If you are working with an Excel table in a workbook, click any cell in the table, click Map on the Insert tab on the ribbon, and then click Launch Power Map. If you are working with a Data Model, click Map on the Insert tab. Either way, a new window displays an empty map in the center of the screen and the field list for your table or Data Model in the right pane. You then select the geographic fields to map, such as City or State Or Province. If Power Map does not automatically recognize the map level, such as Latitude, you can use the drop-down list to the right of the field name to associate the field with the correct map level. Power Map begins plotting data points for these locations on the map, as shown in Figure 4-16. Click the Next button to continue with the map design process.

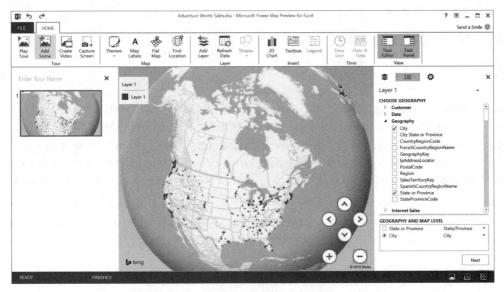

FIGURE 4-16 The creation of a new Power Map and assignment of geographic fields to corresponding map levels.

Visualizing geographic data

After identifying the geographic fields to map, your next step is to explore the data in the map by defining the visualization type to use and the value to assign to the visualization. You choose the visualization type in the Type list, and then, if you are working with the Column visualization type, you assign a value to Height by selecting it in the field list or by dragging it from the field list to the Height box. Power Map automatically aggregates the value you select; it uses Sum by default, but you can change the aggregation function to Average, Count, Max, Min, or None by clicking the arrow icon to the right of the field name and selecting the function you want.

> **Important** Power Map reads the data from the Data Model when you initially create the map. If you make design changes to the model or refresh the data in the model, you must click Refresh Data on the Power Map ribbon to synchronize the map with your underlying data model.

You can enhance the column appearance by adding a field to the Category box. Each distinct value for the field you select is assigned a separate color, and a corresponding legend appears on your map. In addition, Power Map calculates the aggregated values for each geographic field in your data set and plots the values on the map, as shown in Figure 4-17. As the value of the aggregated field increases, the height of the column also increases. You can use the option button next to the Category label in the Task Panel to specify whether the categories should be displayed as a clustered column chart or a stacked column chart. Use the Shapes command on the ribbon to change from a square shape for the column to a different shape, such as a triangle.

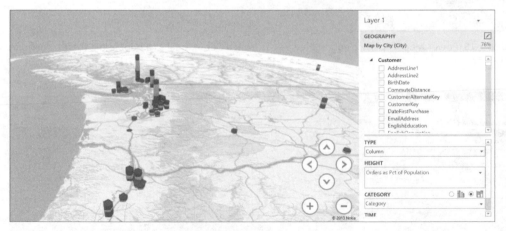

FIGURE 4-17 Power Map displaying aggregated values from a Data Model as a column chart by geographic fields.

At the time of this writing, three additional options are available for visualizing your geographic data:

- **Bubble** You can use the Bubble type to produce a visualization that increases the size of a bubble at a geographical location as the aggregated value assigned to Size increases. If you add a category to the visualization, it switches to a pie chart to display the categories as ratios, as shown in Figure 4-18.

- **Heat map**   When you switch to the HeatMap type, a spectrum of color is associated with the range of aggregated values, with smaller numbers displayed as blue hues and larger numbers displayed as red hues, as shown in Figure 4-19. There is no option to categorize a heat map.

- **Regions**   Rather than display data for a specific geographic location, Power Map can aggregate the values at one of the following levels: country/region, state/province, county, or zip code/postal code. Figure 4-20 shows an example of total sales calculated by state or province worldwide. When this type of chart includes a category, the legend indicates how the opacity of the category color increases as the category represents a higher percentage of the overall value in the geographic region. You can change the options for category shading by clicking the arrow icon to the right of the Category label.

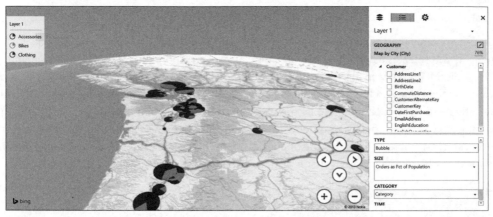

FIGURE 4-18 Power Map displaying aggregated values from a Data Model as a bubble/pie chart by geographic fields.

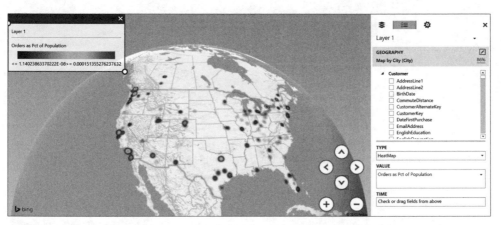

FIGURE 4-19 Power Map displaying aggregated values from a Data Model as a heat map chart by geographic fields.

FIGURE 4-20 Power Map displaying aggregated values from a Data Model as a region chart by state or province.

Regardless of the type of map you create, you can point to a data point to display a dynamic ScreenTip. This ScreenTip includes the geographic details, the aggregated value, and the category label, as shown in Figure 4-21. You cannot customize the ScreenTip to include other data elements.

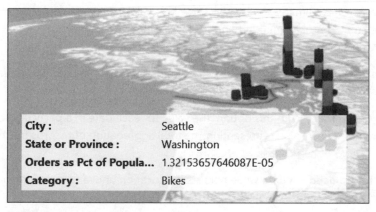

FIGURE 4-21 A ScreenTip in Power Map.

Exploring the 3-D map

Power Map allows you to navigate your map by using a mouse, a keyboard, or both. Table 4-1 lists your navigation options.

TABLE 4-1 Power Map navigation options

To do this	With your mouse, do this	With your keyboard, do this
Zoom closer to a location	Double-click location on the globe	
Zoom in and zoom out	Use scroll wheel	Press the plus (+) or minus (-) key
Pan the globe without pitch change	Click and drag the globe in any direction	Press the up, down, left, or right arrow key
Pan the globe with pitch change	Press the Alt key, and then click and drag the globe in any direction	Press the Alt key, and then press the left or right arrow key to pan with the current pitch, or press the up or down arrow key to alter the pitch
Reset globe	Zoom out completely with scroll wheel	

You can also use the Find Location command on the Power Map ribbon to find a specific location, even if that location is not represented in your data set. After clicking Find, provide one of the following: region, point of interest, or latitude and longitude. Power Map then adjusts the map to your specified location.

Displaying values over time

If you have a field with a date data type in your data, drag it to the Time box in the Task Panel. Click the arrow icon to the right of the field that you added to map the field to one of the following time types: None, Day, Month, Quarter, or Year. When you click Play in the Power Map Time player that appears in the map area, Power Map animates the map to show how values change over time or how values accumulate over time. You control animation behavior by clicking the Settings button next to the Time label in the Task Panel. Your options include:

- **Data Shows For An Instant**   In this case, the visualization of data changes with each date and location combination in the data set.

- **Data Accumulates Over Time**   With this option, the value for each date in a particular location is aggregated, with the final value representing the total aggregation of records for the time series.

- **Data Stays Until It Is Replaced**   A data value persists in a location until a new date record for that location occurs in the time sequence.

Enhancing a map

You can enhance your map in the following ways:

- **Add a two-dimensional (2-D) chart**   To do this, click 2D Chart in the Insert group on the Power Map ribbon. If your map has multiple layers, you must first pick the layer to display in the chart. A chart of the top 100 locations is displayed above the map. You can customize this chart by using the drop-down list in the upper-right corner to change the chart type. If the map contains a category, you can click the category name, such as Bikes in Figure 4-22, to select a different category. You can also toggle to view the bottom 100 locations by clicking the phrase Top 100 in the chart. When you point to the horizontal axis, a scroll bar appears when the entire set of locations can't be viewed in the size allotted to the chart. If you select a bar in the chart, you can see cross-filtering applied to the data on the map.

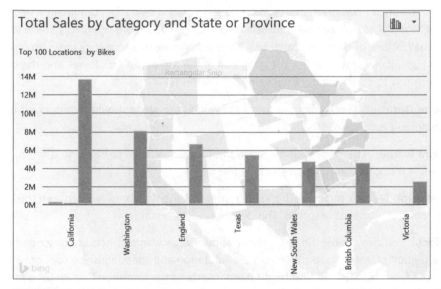

FIGURE 4-22 A 2-D chart superimposed over a map to display the top 100 locations for the current value by category.

- **Add text**   There are two ways to add text to a map. First, you can right-click a data point in the map and select Add Annotation. In the dialog box, you provide a title for the annotation and an optional description. The description can be custom, a selection of fields displayed in the map, or an image. The second way to add text to a map is to insert a text box. The result looks like an annotation, but the text box is not bound to a data point, as an annotation is. You can format the font properties for both a text box and an annotation.

- **Add legend**   When you add a category, Power Map automatically adds a legend. If you remove the legend to see more of the map area, you can add the legend back by clicking Legend on the Power Map ribbon.

- **Apply theme**   Use the Themes command on the Power Map ribbon to apply formatting to the colors and images used in the map. Some images can provide road details, while other images provide a satellite view. If your tour contains multiple scenes, you have the option to use a different theme in each scene.

- **Add map labels** Click Map Labels on the Power Map ribbon to superimpose the names of countries on the map when it is zoomed out. As you zoom in, the labels for states or provinces, cities, and points of interest are displayed.

- **Switch to flat map** For some visualizations, you might find it more helpful to view the data on a flat map. Click Flat Map on the Power Map ribbon to switch between the 3-D view and the flat map view.

Working with tours, scenes, and layers

When you first launch Power Map in a workbook, you create a new tour containing a single scene by default. The initial scene contains only one layer. You can add more layers to a scene to present different visualizations of data simultaneously. Click Add Scene to add scenes to your map and have a collection to play in sequence. Click the gear icon at the top of the Task Panel, and then click the Scene Options link to configure the following scene settings:

- **Scene Duration (Sec)** You can specify how long the scene should be displayed in seconds. The default is six seconds.

- **Scene Name** The name is displayed in the Tour Editor pane to help you distinguish between views. It is not displayed when you play the tour.

- **Transition Duration (Sec)** This value represents the time to move between the locations at the focus of consecutive scenes. The default is three seconds.

- **Effect** You can choose the style of transition. The available effects are described in Table 4-2. The default effect is Station. The transition duration and speed must be configured properly to see the full effect. That is, you might need to extend the transition time or set a faster speed to view the transition before the scene ends.

- **Effect Speed** You can increase or decrease the effect speed by using a slider.

TABLE 4-2 Available transition effects

Effect type	Effect	Description
Circular	Circle	The scene rotates counterclockwise as it centers over the target location.
	Figure 8	The scene moves toward the new location, passes it, and circles back to form a figure 8.
Straight-line	Dolly	The scene moves in a straight line toward the target location.
	Fly Over	The scene moves toward the target location and passes it halfway through the scene.
	Push In	The scene moves toward the target location in a straight line and then zooms in slightly.
Other	Station	This is the default effect. The transition occurs by moving toward the target location, but no additional motion is added to the scene.

When you close a scene in Edit mode, you save its current state. Later, during Playback mode, which you launch by clicking Play Tour on the Power Map ribbon, you can pause a tour and explore the map without stopping the tour. However, any changes you make to a scene in Playback mode are not saved. You can use the Next and Previous buttons to accelerate switching to the next or previous scene.

A workbook can contain multiple tours. When you return to the worksheet view in Excel and later insert a new Power Map, a dialog box displays existing tours for you to open, but it also gives you the option to delete a tour or to add a new one. Using the same dialog box, you can also duplicate a tour to use it as a starting point for a new visualization. Just right-click an existing tour, and select Duplicate Tour.

> **Important** You cannot undo the deletion of a tour.

Sharing Power Map

You can share your map with others who have no access to Power Map by using the Capture Screen or Create Video commands on the Power Map ribbon. The Capture Screen command simply captures an image of your map and places it on the Clipboard so that you can paste it into a document or slide presentation. When you create a video, you must choose one of the following quality levels for the MP4 file format:

- **Presentation & HD Displays**   Use this option for high-definition resolution of 1080p.

- **Computers & Tablets**   This option is best for computer monitors and tablets with a resolution of 720p.

- **Quick Export & Mobile**   This is a small video format for sharing on mobile devices at a resolution of 360p.

> **Note** You can configure the quality of the graphics for the video capture by displaying the File tab and selecting Options. The Power Map Options dialog box displays the following three choices: Speed for lower-quality graphics, Balanced for balancing quality with performance (default), and High Quality for producing higher-quality graphics at a slower speed.

Introducing Power BI for Office 365

Power BI for Office 365 is a new business-intelligence (BI) solution that extends the self-service BI capabilities in Excel. Power BI enables users to share their work in the cloud while maintaining a secure connection to on-premises and cloud-based data sources and allows users to interact with reports in a browser or on a mobile device by accessing a common repository hosted in a special SharePoint site dedicated to Power BI. Users can even designate favorite reports to more easily find the reports they need most often and can get answers from their data by asking natural-language questions.

Power BI also provides a support infrastructure for managing self-service BI in the cloud. A Data Management Gateway provides connectivity to data sources. In addition, designated users can serve as data curators by finding and shaping data in Power Query and then sharing and annotating the query through Power BI.

> **Note** To use Power BI, you must have Power BI for Office 365 E3 or E4, Office 365 ProPlus, or Office Professional Plus 2013 and the Power Map and Power Query add-ins. You can learn how to provision Power BI by following the steps in *How to set up Power BI*, available at *http://go.microsoft.com/fwlink/?LinkId=317870*.

Power BI sites

A Power BI site is a special type of SharePoint Online site that serves as a repository for Excel workbooks that implement Power Pivot, Power Query, Power View, or Power Map. The site also provides a link to the My Power BI site and the Power BI Admin Center. After you subscribe to Power BI for Office 365, you can access the Power BI sites app and apply it to a new or existing site in your SharePoint Online Enterprise environment. At present, only users with a current Power BI for Office 365 subscription can access a Power BI site.

When you publish a workbook to a Power BI site, you save it to a SharePoint document library. Use the Save As command on the File tab in Excel, and then select your SharePoint Online account. You might need to sign in to continue. Typically, you can publish your workbook to your team site, and the Power BI site will automatically include the newly published workbook.

> **Note** Objects and data that are not part of a Data Model cannot exceed 10 megabytes (MB) in size. If you have trouble saving a workbook because of its size, consider modifying or removing tables, images, shaded cells, colored worksheets, text boxes, and clip art.

The Power BI site is a view that restricts the display of documents to Excel workbooks. However, workbooks are not automatically enabled for Power BI. For example, if you upload a workbook to a standard SharePoint document library view, you must then navigate to the Power BI site (using the link in the Quick Launch panel on the left of your screen), click the ellipsis in the lower-right corner of the workbook tile, and then click Enable. In the Enable In Power BI For Office 365 dialog box, click Enable. Alternatively, if you navigate first to the Power BI site and click the Add link to upload your workbook directly to Power BI, it is automatically enabled. Either way, a thumbnail image of your workbook is displayed on the Power BI page soon after the workbook is enabled, as shown in Figure 5-1. The Power BI site can render an enabled workbook as large as 250 MB in the Excel Web App, whereas a standard site prevents the rendering of a workbook that is larger than 30 MB.

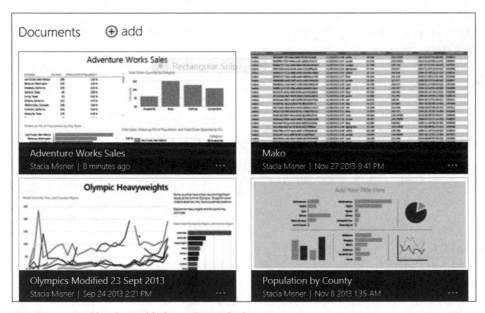

FIGURE 5-1 Workbooks enabled on a Power BI site.

When you click a workbook, the Excel Web App displays the workbook in the browser and allows you to navigate from sheet to sheet. You can interact with PivotTables and PivotCharts by filtering and sorting, but you cannot change the layout of the pivot at this point. Similarly, a Power View sheet allows you to interact by cross-filtering, sorting, and filtering, but you cannot add or modify fields in the report. To fully interact with the workbook, click the right-most icon in the status bar of your browser window, as shown in Figure 5-2, to view the full-size workbook. When you open the full-size workbook, you have access to the Field List for pivots, which lets you make changes online. However, to make changes to Power View reports, you must edit the workbook in Excel. If the Field List is hidden, right-click the PivotChart or PivotTable, and select Show Field List.

FIGURE 5-2 Workbook status bar from which the full-size workbook is accessible.

Configuring featured workbooks

You can designate a maximum of three workbooks as featured workbooks for a Power BI site. Featured workbooks appear at the top of the site's page, above the thumbnail images of the complete set of uploaded workbooks. To feature a workbook, click the ellipsis in the lower-right corner of the workbook tile, and then click Feature. If you select this option for a fourth workbook, that workbook is added as a featured workbook and the first workbook you selected in this process is no longer featured.

Opening Power View in HTML5

Regardless of which mode you use to open your workbook, a button icon is displayed at the lower-right corner of your Power View report, as shown in Figure 5-3. Use this button to display your report in HTML5. At the time of this writing, this feature is in preview mode and subject to change. Because Power View has a Silverlight requirement, the types of devices and browsers that can display a report are limited. With HTML5, the range of possibilities for interacting with reports in a browser interface is expanded.

> **Note** The HTML5 preview will continue to evolve after this writing. For a current set of features supported by Power View in HTML5, see *http://office.microsoft.com/en-us/excel/features-of-the-power-bi-app-and-power-view-in-html5-preview-HA104168262.aspx?CTT=5&origin=HA104149776.*

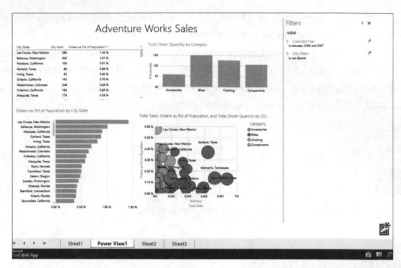

FIGURE 5-3 A Power View report displayed in Power BI with the HTML5 icon in the lower-right corner.

Adding favorite reports to My Power BI

Each user can mark reports as favorites to have them appear in a private site called My Power BI. To do this, click the ellipsis in the lower-right corner of the workbook tile on a Power BI site, and then click Favorite to add it to My Power BI (or Unfavorite to remove it). A star is displayed in the upper-right corner of the thumbnail image as a cue that the report has been marked as a favorite. The report does not move but is tagged for display when you open the My Power BI site. If you have multiple Power BI sites in the same SharePoint Online tenant, you can consolidate reports from these sites into your own My Power BI site. When you have the Power Bi site open, you can click the My Power BI link at the upper-right corner of your browser window to view your reports, as shown in Figure 5-4.

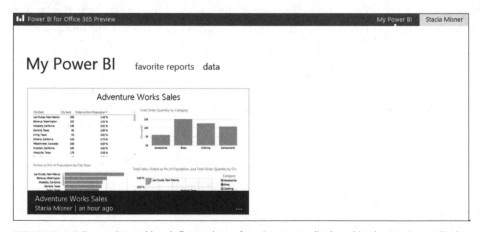

FIGURE 5-4 A Power BI workbook flagged as a favorite report displayed in the My Power BI site.

Shared queries

Self-service BI is only as good as the information that people can find on their own. The purpose of Power BI is to help users find the data they need, obtain access if necessary, and confirm the validity of the data. Shared queries—resources created by some users for others—can fulfill this purpose, but shared queries are managed by data stewards and administrators to ensure that data is being used correctly. Users can work with shared queries in Power Query and then monitor usage analytics in the Manage Data portal.

Creating a shared query

If your organization is using Power BI for Office 365, you can share a query from Power Query by storing the query in the cloud. When you share a query, you save not only the metadata that describes the data source but also the subsequent transformations, so you or others can reuse the steps from that query later. The data resulting from the query's execution is not saved in the cloud as part of the shared query.

To share a query, you must first sign in to Power BI, which you do by clicking Sign In on the Power Query tab on the ribbon. Click Workbook on the Power Query ribbon to view a list of queries in the workbook, right-click the query, and then select Share. In the Share Query dialog box, shown in Figure 5-5, you can modify the name and description of the query. You should take time to provide a meaningful and keyword-rich description to help users find the query through a search. You might prefer to use a Word document to provide a longer description of the query. Rather than typing the description, you can use the Document URL field to specify its location.

FIGURE 5-5 The Share Query dialog box displaying query metadata and sharing settings.

The View In Portal link (which opens the Manage Data portal in SharePoint Online) is displayed in the Data Sources section, which also includes a list of all data sources contributing to the query results. You can review usage analytics online to determine whether the addition of a new shared query is helpful or conflicts with existing queries. This analysis may in turn help you determine how to distinguish your query in the name and description fields.

You must set the sharing settings to grant access to yourself only, to everyone, or to specific Windows logins or Windows security groups. If you are the one sharing the query, you are automatically included and do not need to explicitly add your login to this section.

Another decision you make when creating a shared query is whether to upload rows of data for previewing. If the underlying data source contains sensitive data, you should not select the Upload First Few Rows For Preview check box. Even if a user does not have permissions to access the data source, the query preview results are still visible when a user browses shared queries.

If you are a member of the Data Steward group, you have the option to certify a query. The certification check box is displayed only to members of this group. Certification is an indication that a query has been formally reviewed and accepted for general use and is therefore considered a trusted query.

Using a shared query

When working with Power Query, you can use Online Search to find shared queries, or you can click Shared on the Power Query tab on the ribbon to view a complete list of shared queries. When you point to a shared query in the list, a preview flyout screen appears. To use the query, point to the ellipsis at the bottom of the flyout screen and click Add To Worksheet. If you need to modify the query, click Edit Query on the Query tab under the Table Tools tab on the ribbon.

If you do not have permissions to use a shared query, you see a Request Access link. This link sends an email message to a designated recipient or opens a webpage where you can request access. The data steward responsible for the shared query specifies whether the access request is associated with email or a URL.

Managing query metadata

As a data steward, you can review data sources and manage metadata in the My Power BI site. To do this, click the Data link at the top of the page, and then click Data Sources in the navigation pane. Here you have access to the cloud-based metadata repository for Power BI. As data sources are added, the metadata is often missing, and you see a list of untitled data sources. Click the ellipsis to the right of a data source, click Edit, and then type a display name and a description. In addition, you have the option to provide an email address or a URL for users to contact when they request access to this data source.

Reviewing usage analytics

When your My Power BI site is open, you can use the Data link to open the Manage Data portal.

Another way to access this information is to sign in to Power BI from the Power Query tab in Excel and then click Shared on the ribbon. Point to a query, click the ellipsis at the right of Edit Settings at the bottom of the preview flyout screen, and then click View Statistics. Both of these methods take you to the same location in your Power BI site, the Manage Data portal.

This portal shows the usage analytics for your queries (shown in Figure 5-6), the shared queries you created by using Power Query, and the data sources you have used. This information can help you measure the usefulness of your queries and see whether others have come to rely on those queries. You can assess this information to determine whether it's time to formalize a data source as part of your organization's enterprise information architecture. You can filter the usage analytics to display results for the last day, the last 30 days, or the last year.

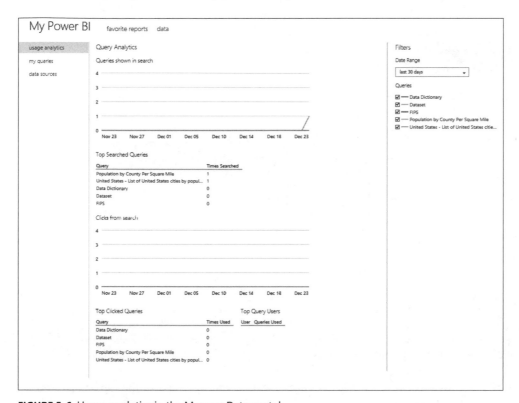

FIGURE 5-6 Usage analytics in the Manage Data portal.

Power BI Q&A

Power BI Q&A is a self-service BI feature available only online. First, you upload a workbook to the Power BI site. Then, you can type your own questions or select from a list of suggested questions. These questions do not require you to learn a specialized query or expression language, however. Instead, you ask questions by using your own words. Q&A automatically selects the best type of visual display for the data it returns from the query, which might be an interactive chart, a map, or a graph.

You can override this behavior by including the name of the visualization that you prefer in the question or by changing the visualization after viewing the selection from Q&A.

To start Q&A, you must have at least one Power BI–enabled workbook uploaded to your Power BI site. Click the ellipsis in the lower-right corner of the workbook tile, and then click Add To Q&A. Next, click the Search With Power BI Q&A link at the upper-right corner of the page. Start typing your question in the balloon that's displayed at the top of the page. Q&A can autocomplete words you enter and displays sample questions that you can use to refine your question further. When you finish the question, Q&A displays the results. You might need to adjust the source workbook by clicking Show More in the navigation pane and selecting a different workbook, as shown in Figure 5-7. To change the current visualization, select one of the items in the Show As list in the navigation pane on the left side of the screen.

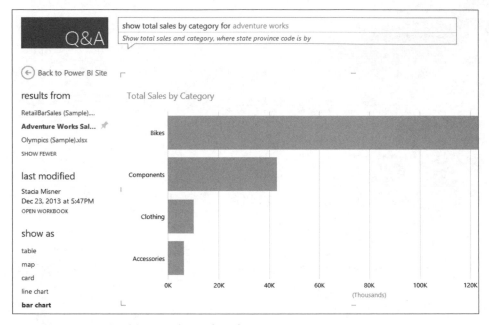

FIGURE 5-7 A Power BI Q&A question and results.

Here are some examples of the types of phrases that you can use with the report pictured throughout this chapter:

- Show total sales by category for Adventure Works

- Which subcategory of bikes has the highest sales?

- Show a list of customers in Washington

Note Because a common idea can be expressed in many ways, you can add synonyms to a data model to help users find information when they do not know the specific names of objects in that model. For more information about working with synonyms, see *http://office.microsoft.com/en-us/excel-help/add-synonyms-to-a-power-pivot-excel-data-model-HA104143188.aspx?CTT=5&origin=HA104149776*. Additionally, there are optimizations to your data that can help improve the search results from Q&A. Learn more about these techniques at *http://office.microsoft.com/en-us/excel-help/enhancing-and-tuning-excel-power-pivot-workbooks-for-power-bi-q-a-HA104143202.aspx?CTT=5&origin=HA104149776*.

Power BI for Mobile

Power BI for Mobile is a touch-optimized Windows 8 app for a tablet. By using this app, you can view any workbook saved to Office 365.

Preparing a workbook for mobile viewing

Power BI for Mobile does not display a workbook in the same way that SharePoint Online does. Instead, it displays a workbook as a set of related pages with one item to a page. An item is a Power View report, a PivotTable, a chart, a PivotChart, or a table. A named range is also an item that is displayed on a separate page, except that other items appearing within the range appear on the same page. You determine which items are displayed online by opening the File tab in Excel, selecting Info, and then clicking Browser View Options. In the Browser View Options dialog box, you can select Sheets or Items in the drop-down list. If you choose Sheets, you can choose to display only Power View reports.

The only control you have over the sequencing of pages is to use a naming convention. Power BI for Mobile displays all items except Power View reports alphabetically by name. Then it displays the Power View reports in the order in which they appear in the workbook.

Important To be visible in the Power BI for Mobile app, your workbook item or sheet must be based on the Excel Data Model in a workbook hosted in Office 365, a Windows Azure SQL Database, or an OData feed. An item or sheet based on any other type of data source will be displayed as a blank page.

Using Power BI for Mobile

When you open the Power BI for Mobile app, swipe up to display the app bar, tap Browse, and then, on the Locations page, swipe up to show the app bar. In the box, type the URL for your SharePoint Online site, and then tap the Go arrow to the right of the URL. You must provide a user name and password to browse your workbooks. Navigate to Shared Documents, and then tap a report. Once a report is open, you can swipe up at any time to access the app bar, where you can tag a report as a favorite or use the Reset To Original button to restore the report to its original state and refresh the data. In addition, you can see thumbnail images of the report, as shown in Figure 5-8, so that you can easily jump to a different page.

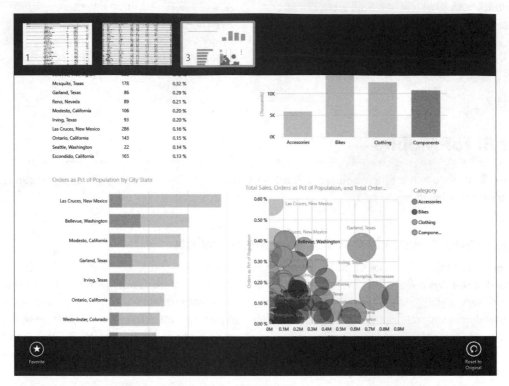

FIGURE 5-8 A Power View report and thumbnails of workbook pages in the Power BI for Mobile app.

The Power BI for Mobile app is designed for an interactive touch experience with the following features in mind for Power View:

- **Highlight** In a Power View sheet, tap a chart element such as a bar, column, or legend item to bring the selected data into view. The other data is displayed with a more subdued hue to help you see the ratio between the two subsets of data. Clear the selection by tapping the chart background. You can select multiple items for highlighting by tapping the icon with three bars in the upper-right corner of the chart.

- **Filter** For any item that has a filter defined, tap the filter icon in the upper-right corner to open the filter pane. You can change filter values and clear the filters, but you cannot add or delete a filter.

- **Zoom** You can pinch and expand your fingers on the tablet's surface to zoom out or in, respectively. However, this technique currently works only on Excel items and not on Power View sheets.

- **Sort a table column**   To sort, tap the column heading in an Excel item. Swipe labels on the horizontal axis of a Power View column chart or the vertical axis on a bar chart.

- **Drill**   You can double-click a field to drill down to the next level of a hierarchy (if one is defined in the data model). Click the Drill Up arrow to return to the previous level.

As long as you leave the Power BI for Mobile app open, the filter and sort selections you have applied remain intact. However, when you close the app, the filter and sort selections are removed.

Sharing a report from Power BI for Mobile

To share a report that you are viewing in the Power BI for Mobile app, swipe from the right, click Share, and then type the email recipient's address. The app sends an email message containing a link to the report rather than the page you are viewing. The recipient can use one of two links to view the report, but only if the recipient already has permissions to view the report in SharePoint Online. The MOBILEBI link connects the user to the report in the Power BI for Mobile app, and the HTTPS link opens the report in a browser window using the Excel Web App.

Power BI administration

Power BI for Office 365 includes an administrative infrastructure that you manage through the Power BI Admin Center. To access the Power BI Admin Center if you are a member of the Admin group, click the Power BI Admin Center link on the Tools menu (gear icon) in the upper-right corner of a Power BI site. From a standard SharePoint Online site, click the Power BI link on the Admin menu in the upper-right corner. This centralized portal for administrative tasks allows you to perform the following tasks:

- **Monitor system health**   Use the System Health page to access logs. You can search by severity, source, start and end dates and times, and keyword. The logs are displayed in a table format in your browser, or you can download current logs as a CSV file. When you point to a message describing an error in the log, a pop-up window displays a link to a help page with instructions to resolve errors and warnings.

- **Manage data gateways**   Use the Gateways page to review a list of existing gateways and their current status. A gateway is the mechanism that securely connects Power BI to an on-premises data source and runs as a client agent on an on-premises computer. When you use this page to set up a new gateway, you download the gateway client, install it locally, and then register the gateway with a key provided in the Power BI Admin Center. You can also use this page to regenerate the key for an existing gateway or to enable the cloud credential store for the gateway so that you can quickly restore the gateway on another computer if the current gateway fails.

- **Configure data sources**   Use the Data Sources page to review a list of existing on-premises data sources and their current status. You can edit, delete, or test the connection for an existing data source. When you edit the data source, you specify whether it is enabled for cloud access, which means workbooks with this data source can be refreshed in SharePoint Online, and whether it is enabled as an OData feed that users can access by using Power Query. You also use the Data Sources page to add a new data source, optionally enable it for cloud access or an OData feed, assign it to a gateway, and specify the connection properties or provide a connection string. Currently, only SQL Server and Oracle are supported as data source types.

- **Define security for administrative roles**   Use the Role Management page to add members to the Admin group, which grants permission to access the Power BI Admin Center, or to the Data Steward group, which grants permission to certify queries for use in Power Query.

- **Specify settings for Power BI**   Use the Settings page to configure general settings such as whether to display top users in the usage analytics dashboard or to enable Windows authentication for OData feeds when the Microsoft Online Directory Synchronization Tool is configured. You can also define the recipients of email notifications and specify whether any of the following events trigger a notification: the expiration of a gateway, the release of a new version of the Data Management Gateway client, or an indexing failure for an OData feed.

Big data solutions

*B*ig data, the term generally used to characterize very large sets of data, has seen increasing use
the past few years. In this chapter, we review the various ways that big data is described and how
Hadoop developed as a technology commonly used to process big data. In addition, we introduce
Microsoft HDInsight, an implementation of Hadoop available as a Windows Azure service. Then we
explore Microsoft PolyBase, an on-premises solution that integrates relational data stored in
Microsoft SQL Server Parallel Data Warehouse (PDW) with nonrelational data stored in a Hadoop
Distributed File System (HDFS).

Big data

For several decades, many organizations have been analyzing data generated by transactional
systems. This data has usually been stored in relational database management systems. A common
step in the development of a business-intelligence solution is weighing the cost of transforming,
cleansing, and storing this data in preparation for analysis against the perceived value that insights
derived from the analysis of the data could deliver. As a consequence, decisions are made about what
data to keep and what data to ignore. Meanwhile, the data available for analysis continues to prolifer-
ate from a broad assortment of sources, such as server log files, social media, or instrument data from
scientific research. At the same time, the cost to store high volumes of data on commodity hardware
has been decreasing, and the processing power necessary for complex analysis of all this data has
been increasing. This confluence of events has given rise to new technologies that support the management and analysis of big data.

Describing big data

The point at which data becomes big data is still the subject of much debate among data-
management professionals. One approach to describing big data is known as the *3Vs*: volume, velocity, and variety. This model, introduced by Gartner analyst Doug Laney in 2001, has been extended
with a fourth V, variability. However, disagreement continues, with some people considering the
fourth V to be veracity.

Although it seems reasonable to associate volume with big data, how is a large volume different
from the very large databases (VLDBs) and extreme workloads that some industries routinely
manage? Examples of data sources that fall into this category include airline reservation systems,
point of sale terminals, financial trading, and cellular-phone networks. As machine-generated data

outpaces human-generated data, the volume of data available for analysis is proliferating rapidly. Many techniques, as well as software and hardware solutions such as PDW, exist to address high volumes of data. Therefore, many people argue that some other characteristic must distinguish big data from other classes of data that are routinely managed.

Some people suggest that this additional characteristic is velocity or the speed at which the data is generated. As an example, consider the data generated by the Large Hadron Collider experiments, which is produced at a rate of 1 gigabyte (GB) per second. This data must be subsequently processed and filtered to provide 30 petabytes (PB) of data to physicists around the world. Most organizations are not generating data at this volume or pace, but data sources such as manufacturing sensors, scientific instruments, and web-application servers are nonetheless generating data so fast that complex event-processing applications are required to handle high-volume and high-speed throughputs. Microsoft StreamInsight is a platform that supports this type of data management and analysis.

Data does not necessarily require volume and velocity to be categorized as big. Instead, a high volume of data with a lot of variety can constitute big data. Variety refers to the different ways that data might be stored: structured, semistructured, or unstructured. On the one hand, data-warehousing techniques exist to integrate structured data (often in relational form) with semistructured data (such as XML documents). On the other hand, unstructured data is more challenging, if not impossible, to analyze by using traditional methods. This type of data includes documents in PDF or Word format, images, and audio or video files, to name a few examples. Not only is unstructured data problematic for analytical solutions, but it is also growing more quickly than file systems on a single server can usually accommodate.

Big data as a branch of data management is still difficult to define with precision, given that many competing views exist and that no clear standards or methodologies have been established. Data that looks big to one organization by any of the definitions we've described might look small to another organization that has evolved solutions for managing specific types of data. Perhaps the best definition of big data at present is also the most general. For the purposes of this chapter, we take the position that big data describes a class of data that requires a different architectural approach than the currently available relational database systems can effectively support, such as append-only workloads instead of updates.

Exploring the history of Hadoop

Any research into potential architectural solutions for managing big data inevitably leads to a mention of Hadoop, a technology whose first iteration, dubbed Nutch, was developed by Doug Cutting and Mike Cafarella in 2002 as a way to crawl and index webpages across the Internet. Nutch, however, had limited scalability and was prone to fail. After Google released the Google File System paper in 2003 and the MapReduce paper in 2004, Cutting and Cafarella were inspired to design a distributed file system and MapReduce processing framework that gave more scalability and reliability to Nutch.

When Cutting joined Yahoo in 2006, the storage and processing components of Nutch were separated and contributed to the Apache Software Foundation as an open-source software project named Hadoop (after a toy elephant belonging to Cutter's son). Even then, the focus of Hadoop was to facilitate web searches, but its scalability and reliability remained limited. Ongoing investment by Yahoo increased scalability from dozens of nodes to thousands over a period of several years. Meanwhile, Yahoo began storing more and more data in Hadoop and allowed data scientists to research and analyze this data, which provided the feedback necessary to develop new applications and attain a greater level of maturity in the platform. Externally, the open-source status of Hadoop attracted attention from academics and investors as a general-purpose computing platform more than for its origins as a web search engine.

Hadoop is attractive for general use because of its scale-out architecture on commodity hardware and its support for parallel processing on a large scale. As an Apache open-source project, Hadoop is not a software application but rather a framework consisting of multiple modules:

- **Hadoop Common package** Java libraries and utilities necessary to run Hadoop modules, source code, and documentation.

- **Hadoop Distributed File System (HDFS)** A distributed file system that replicates large files across multiple nodes in case of potential hardware failure. A file is split into blocks, and then each block is copied to multiple machines. A centralized metadata store called the *name node* contains the locations for each part of a file.

- **MapReduce engine** A programming framework that supports distributed processing of jobs in parallel within a cluster of server nodes. A MapReduce program requires a *Map()* procedure to perform a specific task across multiple nodes, such as a word count, and a *Reduce()* procedure to consolidate the results from these nodes in summary form. The engine automatically manages distributed processing by partitioning the data to be processed, scheduling the job across nodes, assigning an alternate node if an assigned node fails, and then aggregating the results from each node into a single result.

- **Hadoop YARN** A resource-management platform that controls resources and schedules user applications for Hadoop 2.0 distributions and higher.

From a data-management perspective, one of the distinguishing features of Hadoop as it relates to large data volumes is the movement of processing logic to the data, rather than moving the data to a location where it is processed. Consider a data-warehouse solution in which data is extracted from one or more sources and moved to a new location after transformations have been applied to cleanse and restructure the data. Moving 1 PB of data across a 1-GB network into a data warehouse takes time and consumes network bandwidth. In a Hadoop implementation, after data is added to HDFS, the data remains in place, the processing moves to the data, and only the results of the processing are sent back to the user.

Several Apache open-source projects related to Hadoop are useful for data warehousing and BI applications that rely on a Hadoop implementation:

- **Pig** An infrastructure that uses a scripting language called Pig Latin to generate MapReduce jobs that read data from HDFS, transform data (through filtering, grouping, merging, or splitting the data, for example), and output the results to the console or to HDFS. Learn more at *http://www.windowsazure.com/en-us/documentation/articles/hdinsight-use-pig*.

- **Hive** A data-warehouse solution made up of a metastore that facilitates access to data stored in HDFS through a scripting language called HiveQL. HiveQL is syntactically similar to SQL, with which database professionals are already familiar. Additional information is available at *http://www.windowsazure.com/en-us/documentation/articles/hdinsight-use-hive*.

- **Sqoop** A set of utilities that uses MapReduce and parallelized operations to move data in either direction between Hadoop and a relational database. Read details about Sqoop at *http://www.windowsazure.com/en-us/documentation/articles/hdinsight-upload-data*.

- **Oozie** A workflow manager that allows you to schedule MapReduce, Pig, Hive, and Sqoop jobs by using hPDL, an XML Process Definition Language used to define workflows. You can read about it at *http://www.windowsazure.com/en-us/documentation/articles/hdinsight-use-oozie*.

HDInsight

HDInsight is a Hadoop-based platform that you can use to process data of all kinds in the cloud. In particular, HDInsight is useful for processing high volumes of structured and unstructured data, which traditional relational database systems typically cannot support for a variety of reasons. HDInsight allows you to quickly establish an infrastructure for big data analysis, whether you want to develop a proof of concept for a big data solution or support ongoing analytical requirements in a production environment. Furthermore, HDInsight integrates with Microsoft's business-intelligence tools to enable users to enhance big data with additional sources and then explore and analyze the results to gain deeper insights.

One of the benefits of using a service such as HDInsight is the ability to leave your data at rest in the cloud by using Windows Azure Blob Storage. You can then provision an HDInsight cluster during the time required to process the data and delete the cluster when processing is complete. That way, you do not need to purchase hardware, acquire and install software, and maintain an infrastructure for proofs of concept or short-term projects. Furthermore, its presence in the cloud means that HDInsight can be kept up to date with a current version of Hadoop. On the other hand, frequently upgrading Hadoop in a large enterprise and maintaining components of the entire Hadoop stack can be challenging. As another consideration, if you need to repeatedly process data that is 1 PB or more in size, or if your company already has a large investment in Hadoop, an on-premises solution is typically more cost-effective. Last, if maximal performance is imperative, an on-premises solution is likely a better choice because HDInsight resides in a shared resource environment and therefore cannot deliver a consistent performance experience.

Most functionality within HDInsight and other Hadoop distributions is similar. Consequently, any current experience with Hadoop is largely transferable. Keep in mind that interaction with HDInsight requires you to use Windows Azure PowerShell commands, so a basic knowledge of PowerShell is required to work with the cluster.

Creating a storage account for HDInsight

You can incorporate big data analysis into your business-intelligence solutions by designing an analytical architecture that includes both your enterprise data warehouse (EDW) and HDInsight. HDInsight and related tools, such as Hive and Power BI, are useful for preliminary analysis to determine whether your data contains any valuable insights. If you discover data that is useful for answering questions on an ongoing basis, you can automate extractions from HDInsight to load data into your EDW.

Before you provision a new HDInsight cluster, you must create a Windows Azure Storage account in an active Windows Azure subscription. To do this, click New in the lower-left corner of the Windows Azure portal, click Data Services, click Storage, and then click Quick Create. Type a unique name for the URL of the storage account, select a location, and specify whether you want locally redundant or geo-redundant storage (that is, replicated to nodes in the same region or replicated additionally to a secondary region), as shown in Figure 6-1. Click Create Storage Account at the bottom of the page.

> **Note** For a step-by-step tutorial that teaches you more about Windows Azure and HDInsight, refer to *http://www.windowsazure.com/en-us/documentation/articles/hdinsight-get-started/*.

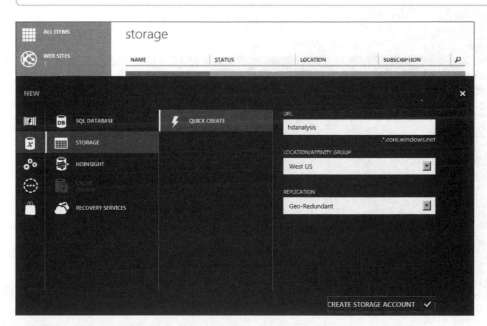

FIGURE 6-1 Creating a Windows Azure Storage account.

When the status of the new storage account changes to Online, click the account name in the list, and then click Manage Access Keys at the bottom of the page. Take note of the account name and primary access key for the storage account. This information is required when you provision your HDInsight cluster. Click the check mark at the bottom of the dialog box to close it.

Provisioning an HDInsight cluster

To provision a cluster by using the Windows Azure portal, click HDInsight at the left, and then click Create An HDInsight Cluster. Type a name for the cluster, select a cluster size, provide an administrator password, and specify the storage account to associate with the cluster, as shown in Figure 6-2. The cluster is created at the same location as the storage account. The status of the cluster changes to Running when it is ready to use.

> **Note** If you want to specify a different number of nodes for cluster size than the list displays, or if you want to assign an administrator name other than "admin," you can use the Custom Create option described at *http://www.windowsazure.com/en-us/documentation/articles/hdinsight-provision-clusters/*. If you later want to increase the number of nodes in your cluster, you can delete the cluster and create a larger one without losing data.

> **Important** You cannot later change the assignment of the storage account to the cluster. If you delete the storage account, the cluster is no longer available.

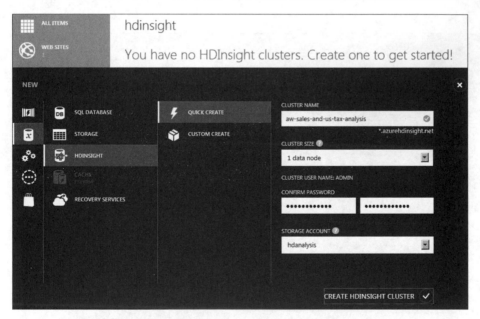

FIGURE 6-2 Creating an HDInsight cluster.

Loading data into a storage account

To work with data in HDInsight, you must first load one or more files, known as *blobs*, into your storage account. More specifically, you load blobs into containers that you create within a storage account, as shown in Figure 6-3. Within a storage account, you can create as many containers as you need. Furthermore, there is no limit on the number of blobs that you can add to a container. The type of blob you add to a container determines how Windows Azure Storage manages both storage and operations. You can add the following blob types:

- **Block blob**   This blob type is useful for most types of document, text, and image files; for streaming audio or video; and for HDInsight. The size of a single blob must be under 200 GB and cannot contain more than 50,000 blocks. Each block can store up to 4 MB of data. A client application manages the deconstruction of a blob into blocks and uploads the blocks in parallel for faster performance. The application also retries the operation for a single block if it fails to upload correctly.

- **Page blob**   This blob type is optimal for random read-write operations. A page blob consists of 512-byte pages that cannot exceed 1 terabyte (TB). A client application writes one or more pages as a new blob or updates an existing blob by appending data to storage.

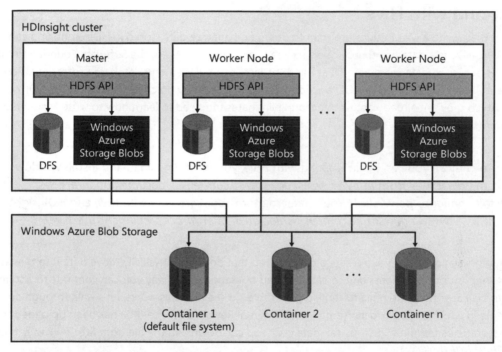

FIGURE 6-3 HDInsight storage architecture.

There are many ways to load data into storage. One way to work with your storage account is to download and install Azure Storage Explorer, available at *http://azurestorageexplorer.codeplex.com*. You must specify the storage account name and provide the storage account key to connect it to your Windows Azure Storage account. You can use Azure Storage Explorer to create a container for blobs, or you can use the Windows Azure management portal, although a default container exists when you initially provision the storage account for use as HDInsight's default file system. Although Azure Storage Explorer provides a simple interface for uploading data, no comparable functionality is provided through the Windows Azure management portal.

Note Other options for loading data into HDInsight include AzCopy, Windows Azure PowerShell, Hadoop command line, and Sqoop. These are described at *http://www.windowsazure.com/en-us/documentation/articles/hdinsight-upload-data/*. For greater control over blob-storage management, you can develop a custom application by using one of many client libraries that wrap the REST interface for Windows Azure Blob Storage service. You can learn more about the REST API for blobs at *http://msdn.microsoft.com/en-us/library/windowsazure/dd135733.aspx*. If you have a lot of data to upload, you might find it more effective with respect to time and cost to send your data on an external hard drive to the data center. Details are available at *http://www.windowsazure.com/en-us/manage/services/storage/import-export-service-for-blob-storage*.

Working with Hive

Rather than write a MapReduce program to query and analyze data stored in HDInsight, you can use Hive. Hive is a data warehouse open-source project under the Apache Software Foundation that enables access to data stored in HDFS. This approach is popular among database professionals because it allows them to use HiveQL, a scripting language that is syntactically similar to the SQL queries with which they are already accustomed, and eliminates the need to learn how to write MapReduce programs in Java.

Note Before you can begin working with Hive, you must download and install Windows Azure PowerShell from *http://www.windowsazure.com/en-us/documentation/articles/install-configure-powershell/*. You can learn more about working with Hive and HDInsight at *http://www.windowsazure.com/en-us/documentation/articles/hdinsight-use-hive/*.

In general, you use Hive to create a table, a step that does not physically move data into the table but rather imposes a schema on the data for read operations. That way you can continue to add more files to HDFS without the need to rebuild your table. To see how this works, let's walk through an example in which 2008 tax data from the U.S. Internal Revenue Service (IRS) has been uploaded to blob storage as tax/data/2008-us-tax-data.csv. (You can download the file from *http://www.irs.gov/pub/irs-soi/08zpall.csv*.)

To run HiveQL queries, you must open a Windows Azure PowerShell console window. Then, connect to your Windows Azure subscription by running the following command and responding to the subsequent prompt with your login credentials:

```
Add-AzureAccount
```

Update the following PowerShell script with the subscription, storage account, container, and cluster names applicable to your HDInsight cluster, and then run the script:

```
$subscriptionName = "<mySubscription>"
$storageAccountName = "<myStorageAccount>"
$containerName = "<myContainer>"
$clusterName = "<myHDInsightCluster>"
```

Run the following script to connect to the correct subscription and cluster before issuing Hive queries:

```
Select-AzureSubscription $subscriptionName
Use-AzureHDInsightCluster $clusterName
```

To update the Hive metadata store with a schema describing the tax data, create and execute the following script:

```
Invoke-Hive -Query "CREATE EXTERNAL TABLE irs_tax_data (
    state string,
    zipcode string,
    agi_class int,
    n1 int,
    mars2 int,
    prep int,
    n2 int,
    numdep int,
    a00100 int,
    a00200 int,
    a00300 int,
    a00600 int,
    a00900 int,
    a23900 int,
    a01400 int,
    a01700 int,
    a02300 int,
    a02500 int,
    a03300 int,
    a04470 int,
    a18425 int,
    a18450 int,
    a18500 int,
    a18300 int,
    a19300 int,
    a19700 int,
    a04800 int,
    a07100 int,
    af5695 int,
    a07220 int,
    a07180 int,
    a59660 int,
    a59720 int,
    a09600 int,
```

```
     a06500 int,
     a10300 int,
     a11900gt0 int,
     a11900lt0 int)
ROW FORMAT DELIMITED
   FIELDS TERMINATED BY ',' 
   LINES TERMINATED BY '\n'
STORED AS TEXTFILE;"
```

It is important to understand that the previous script did not move data into a table. Instead, it serves only as a description of the data that you place in an HDFS directory. You can then load one or more files into that directory and use Hive queries to retrieve data from those files as though they were a single table. To associate the HDFS directory with the external table schema in the default container and storage account, execute the following script:

```
Invoke-Hive -Query "LOAD DATA INPATH 'wasb://$containerName@$storageAccountName.blob.core.
windows.net/tax/data' INTO TABLE irs_tax_data;"
```

Working with CSV output

When you use Hive to output data to a CSV file, the first several rows in the file contain Hive status messages that cause errors when you attempt to import the data into Power Query. You can use the following script to remove these header rows:

```
#Prep File
$File = "c:\temp\irs_tax_data_summary.csv"
#Remove lines
$FileContent = gc $File
$FileContent = $FileContent[5..($FileContent.Count - 2)]
$FileContent | Out-File c:\temp\irs_tax_data_summary_final.csv
```

Analyzing data from Hive

Once data is accessible through Hive, you can work with the data in a number of ways for analytical purposes. For example, you can execute a PowerShell script that runs a Hive query to retrieve summarized results from a table. You can then store the results as a table by using Hive's CREATE TABLE AS SELECT statement or output the results as a CSV file that you save to HDFS or to your local computer. You might save the results as a table when you want to share the results with other users and need to query and analyze the results repeatedly. When the result is relatively small and you are performing a onetime analysis, you might use the CSV file as a quick way to access the data. Yet another option is to use the Hive ODBC driver that you can download from *http://www.microsoft.com/en-us/download/details.aspx?id=40886*.

An example of working with the Hive ODBC driver is to set up a data source name (DSN) on your computer and then reference this DSN when you create a connection in Excel to query the Hive table. To set up the DSN, open Control Panel on your computer, open Administrative Tools, and then open the ODBC Data Source Administrator (using the 32-bit or 64-bit version, as applicable to your operating system). Click the Add button, select Microsoft Hive ODBC Driver in the list, and click Finish. In the Microsoft Hive ODBC Driver DSN Setup dialog box, type a name in the Data Source Name box. In the Host box, type the name of your HDInsight cluster and append **.azurehdinsight.net**, as shown in Figure 6-4. Next, type **admin** in the User Name box (unless you set up an alternative name for the administrator of your HDInsight cluster), and then enter the password that you created for this account. Click the Test button to ensure that you can connect successfully, and then click OK twice to close each dialog box.

FIGURE 6-4 Configuring the Hive ODBC Driver DSN for HDInsight.

To continue the example with tax data stored in a Hive table, you can create a query to import all or part of the Hive table into Excel by using one of the following methods:

- **Microsoft Query Wizard**   You can launch this wizard from the Data tab on the Excel ribbon by clicking From Other Sources and then clicking From Microsoft Query. Select the DSN you created for Hive, clear the Use The Query Wizard check box, and then click OK. You must provide the password for the admin user before you can create the query. Add the irs_tax_data table to the query, and then click the SQL button to define a query. Click OK to save the query, and then click OK to continue when a message is displayed indicating that the SQL query cannot be represented graphically. On the File menu, click Return Data To Microsoft Excel. In the Import Data dialog box, keep the default selection of Table, and then click OK. The wizard adds a table to the worksheet and loads it with data from your query. You are then free to use the data in Excel as you like, but if you later want to add the table to the Excel Data Model, you must manually remove the blank first row. You can then click Add To Data Model on the Power Pivot tab on the ribbon.

- **Power Pivot** On the Power Pivot tab in Excel, click Manage, click From Other Sources, click Others (OLEDB/ODBC), and then click Next. Replace Custom with a friendly name, and then click Build. On the Provider page of the Data Link Properties dialog box, select Microsoft OLE DB Providers For ODBC Drivers, click Next, select Use Connection String, and then click Build. Select the Hive DSN on the Machine Data Source page, click OK, type the admin password for the cluster, click OK, select the Allow Saving Password check box, click OK, and then click Next. Click Next again, and then choose whether to select all data from a table or write a query. When you click Finish after selecting a table or entering a query, Power Pivot executes a query and returns results to the workbook's data model.

Note At the time of writing, Power Query does not include a connection for Hive. You can connect to HDInsight directly, but you can only view the set of files on HDFS. If you save multiple files to a common directory for which you create an external Hive table, you could use Power Query to merge these files, but you cannot retrieve them in a single step by querying the table, as you can with the Microsoft Query Wizard or Power Pivot.

As an example, you might want to summarize the tax data further before importing it into Excel. Whether you import the data using the Microsoft Query Wizard, Power Query, or Power Pivot, a query that retrieves the number of returns (in column n1) and average adjusted gross income (AGI) (in column a00100) by state and by zip code looks like this:

```
SELECT state, zipcode, SUM(n1), ROUND(AVG(a00100/n1),2)
FROM irs_tax_data
GROUP BY state, zipcode LIMIT 100000
```

Note To better understand the tax data example in this chapter, you can download a data dictionary for the tax data from *http://www.irs.gov/file_source/pub/irs-soi/zipcode08flds.xls*.

Note If you add aliases to the expressions in your query, the Hive ODBC driver does not return the alias names as column headers. Additionally, at the time of this writing, the query fails unless you include the LIMIT operator at the end of the SELECT statement.

After you add data from a Hive table to a data model, you can use any of Excel's analytical tools to explore the results. At a minimum, you can create a PivotTable or PivotChart. For more advanced analysis, you can add other data sources and DAX calculations to the data model. For example, let's say that Adventure Works wants to compare the average income of its customers by state and zip code with the average income of taxpayers in the United States by state and zip code. To do this, you can import the DimCustomer table from AdventureWorksDW2012 (which you can download from the SQL Server 2012 DW link accessible at *http://msftdbprodsamples.codeplex.com*), rename it as Customers, change the data types to whole numbers for the returns and adjusted AGI columns, rename those columns by using a more user-friendly name, create a relationship between the tax data table (renamed as Tax) and the Customers table based on the zip code, and optionally add a hierarchy to each table to support navigation from state to zip code. To support comparisons of income levels, you can add DAX calculations to the data model (in the Calculation Area below a table in the Power Pivot window), as shown in Table 6-1.

TABLE 6-1 Sample DAX calculations.

Table	Calculated field to add
Customers	`Average Customer Income:=average([YearlyIncome])`
Tax	`Average AGI:=calculate(average([AGI]), Filter(Tax, [Average Customer Income] >0))`
	`Income Variance:=if(isblank([Average Customer Income]), blank(), -1 * ([Average AGI]-[Average Customer Income])))`
	`Income Variance Pct:=if(isblank([Average AGI]), blank(), [Income Variance]/ [Average AGI])`

With these calculations in place, you can visualize the data with charts and maps, as shown in Figure 6-5. In this example, three visualizations of the Income Variance Pct are displayed in a Power View report. The first visualization is a column chart sorting the values in ascending order. Adventure Works could use this visualization to identify the states where the average income of its customers is significantly lower than the average income reported on tax returns within a state. This disparity might indicate the existence of a large untapped market of potential customers with more disposable income available for buying Adventure Works products. When a hierarchy of states and zip codes exists, a user can double-click a column to view the zip codes associated with the selected state. In the map visualization, the size of each bubble indicates the relative difference between customer and general population income. As the difference increases, the size of the bubble becomes smaller. The visualization that looks like a table is actually a matrix for which the Show Levels option on the Power View Design tab is set to Rows—Enable Drill Down One Level At A Time to support a view of the data by state or by zip code within a selected state.

Power Map offers another way to view this type of data, as shown in Figure 6-6. In this visualization, the geographic data is in the state column in the Tax table and the chart type is set to Region. The legend shows that as the color used within a region becomes lighter, the value of Income Variance Pct is lower. No data exists for the states that have no color. The visualization is displayed as a flat map for easier viewing of the United States.

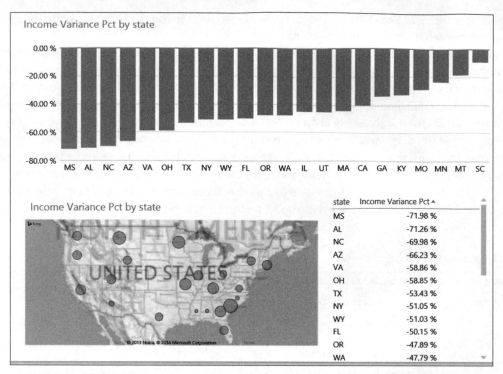

state	Income Variance Pct ▲
MS	-71.98 %
AL	-71.26 %
NC	-69.98 %
AZ	-66.23 %
VA	-58.86 %
OH	-58.85 %
TX	-53.43 %
NY	-51.05 %
WY	-51.03 %
FL	-50.15 %
OR	-47.89 %
WA	-47.79 %

FIGURE 6-5 Power View visualizations of data combined from Hive and SQL Server tables.

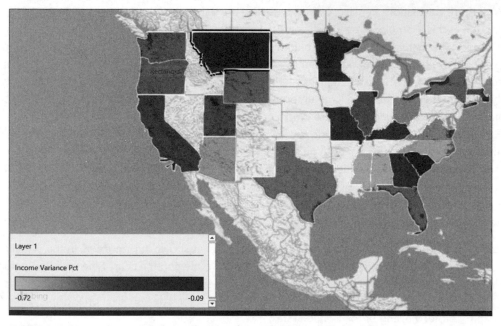

FIGURE 6-6 Power Map regional visualization of Income Variance Pct by state.

PolyBase

PolyBase was developed at the Microsoft Jim Gray Systems Lab at the University of Wisconsin-Madison under the direction of Dr. David DeWitt, a Microsoft Technical Fellow. It provides an interface that allows you to work with data stored in HDFS by using SQL syntax in PDW queries—in a manner similar to querying a linked server from SQL Server—rather than MapReduce jobs. You can even use PolyBase to join relational data in PDW with data in HDFS, as shown in Figure 6-7. In addition, you can use PolyBase to move data from PDW to HDFS or vice versa. Furthermore, you can use Power Query or Power Pivot to connect to PDW and use PolyBase to import data from HDFS into Excel.

> **Note** To learn more about PolyBase, see "Split Query Processing in PolyBase," at *http://gsl. azurewebsites.net/Portals/0/Users/Projects/polybase/PolybaseSigmod2013.pdf.*

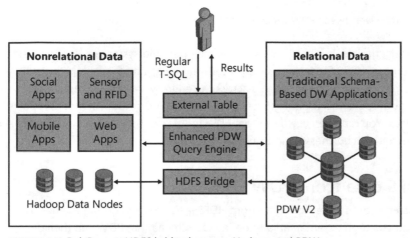

FIGURE 6-7 PolyBase as HDFS bridge between Hadoop and PDW.

Exploring the benefits of PolyBase

The most obvious benefit of the availability of PolyBase in PDW is the ability to combine both relational and nonrelational data into a single result set, but there are several others. In particular, database professionals already familiar with developing SQL queries to retrieve data from PDW for reporting and analytical applications have nothing new to learn when they need to query nonrelational data. There is no need to learn MapReduce, nor is there any need to learn how to use the other tools in the Hadoop ecosystem, such as HiveQL, Pig, or Sqoop. Existing SQL skills are sufficient.

Another benefit is faster results from queries to HDFS. PolyBase is able to perform read and write operations in parallel much faster by taking advantage of the massively parallel processing (MPP) of PDW. Whereas using Sqoop is effective for moving data into and out of a relational database, it processes data serially and interfaces with the PDW control node. By contrast, PolyBase not only parallelizes data transfers but also moves data directly from Hadoop data nodes to PDW compute nodes, as shown in Figure 6-8.

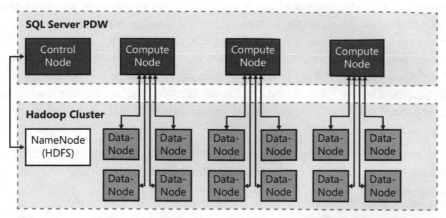

FIGURE 6-8 Parallel data transfer between PDW compute nodes and Hadoop data nodes.

Last, PolyBase is highly flexible. It is not limited to a single operating system or Hadoop distribution. In addition, any type of HDFS file format is supported. This means that you can use PolyBase to deliver data from all types of unstructured sources across the entire Microsoft BI stack. You can connect to PDW with ad hoc analysis tools like Excel and Power BI or distribute standard reports by using Reporting Services. You can even use data from PDW in Analysis Services multidimensional or tabular models to enrich it with business logic and other BI features.

Accessing HDFS data from PDW

The work that PolyBase performs to retrieve data from HDFS is transparent during queries. The only requirement is that you create an external table to define the schema that PDW can then query. You can then interact with data in HDFS files in multiple ways, either by moving data between systems or by querying both systems and joining the results.

Let's say you want to export data from a PDW table called FactInventory and store the results in a text file on your on-premises Hadoop cluster. You use Create Table As Select syntax to create an external table and transfer data from PDW into a file in HDFS, like this:

```
CREATE EXTERNAL TABLE FactInventory_Export
WITH
(LOCATION = hdfs://10.10.10.100:8020/data/FactInventory_Export.txt,
FORMAT OPTIONS (FIELD_TERMINATOR = '|')
AS SELECT * FROM FactInventory;
```

Another option is to create an external table that references data already stored in HDFS, as in this example:

```
CREATE EXTERNAL TABLE ServerLogs(
  machineName varchar(50),
  eventDate date,
  event varchar(100)
)
WITH (
  LOCATION = hdfs://10.10.10.100:8020/data/logs.txt',
  FORMAT_OPTIONS(
    FIELD_TERMINATOR='|',
    DATE_FORMAT = 'MM/dd/yyyy'
  )
)
```

You can then write queries that reference both PDW and external tables pointing to HDFS, as shown here:

```
SELECT sl.machineName, m.machineDescription, m.machineStartDate, sl.eventDate, sl.event
FROM ServerLogs sl
JOIN DimMachine m
ON sl.machineName = m.machineName
```

Index

Numbers

A

B

C

About the authors

 **ROSS MISTRY** is a transformational leader, best-selling author, national director at Microsoft, former SQL Server MVP, and disruptive innovator from the Silicon Valley.

Ross has been a trusted advisor and consultant for many C-level executives and has been responsible for successfully creating technology roadmaps, including the design and implementation of complex technology solutions, for some of the largest companies in the world. He has taken on the lead architect role for many Fortune 50 and Silicon Valley organizations, including Network Appliance, McAfee, EBay, Sharper Image, CIBC, Wells Fargo, and Intel.

Currently, Ross is a national director at Microsoft, responsible for the Microsoft Technology Center (MTC) program in Canada. He recently designed and launched the first MTC in Toronto and is leading a team of enterprise architects. The MTC is a $22 million investment that includes a 20,000-square-foot collaborative environment providing access to innovative technologies and world-class expertise that enables enterprise customers to envision, design, and deploy solutions to meet their exact needs.

Ross has developed a solid reputation as a respected voice for valuable feedback to Microsoft's engineering, sales, and marketing groups. He has helped Microsoft shape products such as SQL Server and Windows Server by representing its customers as the company's central teams design, develop, and deliver new product features, licensing models, and go-to-market strategies.

Ross is an active participant in the worldwide technology community. He comanaged the SQL Server Twitter account and frequently speaks at technology conferences around the world. He has recently spoken at TechReady, TechEd, SQL PASS Community Summit, SQL Connections, and SQL Bits. He is a series author and has written many whitepapers and articles for Microsoft, SQL Server Magazine, and Techtarget.com. Ross's latest books include *SQL Server 2012 Management and Administration, 2nd Edition* (Sams Publishing, 2012), *Introducing Microsoft SQL Server 2012* (Microsoft Press, 2012), and *Windows Server 2008 R2 Unleashed* (Sams Publishing, 2010).

You can follow him on Twitter at @RossMistry or contact him at *http://www.rossmistry. com*.

 **STACIA MISNER** is a consultant, educator, mentor, author, and SQL Server MVP specializing in business-intelligence solutions since 1999. During that time, she has authored or coauthored multiple books about BI. Her latest books include *Microsoft SQL Server Reporting Services 2012* (Microsoft Press, 2013) and *Business Intelligence in Microsoft SharePoint 2013* (Microsoft Press, 2013). Stacia provides consulting and custom education services through her company, Data Inspirations; speaks frequently at conferences serving the SQL Server community; and serves as the chapter leader of her local PASS user group, SQL Server Society of Las Vegas. She is also a contributing editor for SQL Server Pro magazine. Stacia writes about her experiences with BI at *blog.datainspirations.com* and tweets as @StaciaMisner.

Now that you've read the book...

Tell us what you think!

Was it useful?
Did it teach you what you wanted to learn?
Was there room for improvement?

Let us know at http://aka.ms/tellpress

Your feedback goes directly to the staff at Microsoft Press,
and we read every one of your responses. Thanks in advance!